SILVER AND POLITICS
IN NEVADA: 1892‑1902

SILVER
AND POLITICS
IN NEVADA:
1892-1902

by Mary Ellen Glass

UNIVERSITY OF NEVADA PRESS

Reno, Nevada · 1969

University of Nevada Press
Reno, Nevada

© 1969 by University of Nevada Press
Library of Congress Catalog Card Number: 72–92547

Designed by James Mennick
Manufactured in the United States of America
SBN 87417–026–5

For Al, who loves Nevada as much as I do

Preface

MONETARY policy and politics have been inextricably intertwined in the United States since the earliest days of the Republic. Indeed, some of the most outstanding events in United States political history have involved maneuvering, dealing, and ultimately legislating on financial questions. By the 1890s, with the government over a hundred years old, the issues—far from being settled—became perhaps as important as they had ever been in the century-old debates. As the nineteenth century entered its last decade, however, the problems turned not solely on broad economic subjects, but on the metal coinage of the nation and its effect on the financial order. The so-called Populist Revolt of the 1880s and 1890s added fervor and color to the disputes that erupted, and turned the eyes of the country to the western region, where metals and mining had become, in some areas, the basis of the economy.

Nevada contained an outstanding example of the ferment

that erupted over the coinage question. There, the decline of the great Comstock lode, in combination with the most difficult features of recurring national and local economic depressions, caused a political outbreak of unusual proportions. After failing to bring about a desired inflation of the national currency through remonetization of silver, Nevadans turned to an extravagant—and ultimately unsuccessful—action: the politicians put together a new organization and called it the Silver Party of Nevada. This book represents an attempt to reconstruct the political history of the Silver party's decade in power.

I sincerely appreciate the assistance I have received in preparation of this work. Professor Russell R. Elliott of the University of Nevada Department of History has been a constant inspiration. He read, and offered many valuable suggestions for, the manuscript. I am also grateful to Professor James W. Hulse for perceptive and useful comments.

A joint grant from the University of Nevada Center for Western North American Studies and the University of Nevada Library allowed me to purchase from the Yale University Library microfilm copies of a portion of the Francis G. Newlands papers. This material was exceptionally useful; I acknowledge the grant gratefully. I also thank the Yale University Library for permission to use the Newlands papers.

The bulk of the research for this work was done at the University of Nevada Library, the Nevada Historical Society Library, the Nevada State Division of Archives, and the Nevada State Library. In every case, the staffs of these institutions helped me to use their facilities and searched for materials far more than could have been expected as a duty. I thank them all warmly, with a special added "thank

{

you" for many extra favors to the staff of the Nevada Historical Society. The pictures marked UNL are from the collection of the University of Nevada Library in Reno, and those marked NHS are from the Nevada Historical Society.

For editorial assistance, I thank Mrs. Mauriça G. Osborne, who spent many hours and gave dozens of helpful suggestions. I am also grateful to Mrs. Ruth G. Hilts for useful observations on the manuscript. Another grateful acknowledgment goes to the staff of the University of Nevada Press for help in this work.

Finally, I owe a note of appreciation to my family. A wife and mother who does this kind of work is sometimes a burden, but my husband and sons have borne their frustration cheerfully and made my work all the more rewarding. The errors, inadequacies, or omissions in this book are mine alone.

M.E.G.

Reno, Nevada
March 1969

Contents

Introduction: Nevada Profile

NEVADA! The name of the Union's thirty-sixth state has rung joyously or ominously or in tune with jingling coins to the ears of thousands of American citizens. Few residents of the United States are unaware of, or are without opinion upon, this commonwealth which has been many things to as many people.

Nevada's area is about 110,000 square miles, making this far western state the nation's seventh-largest. Because it lies mostly in the so-called Great Basin, the region's rivers and streams run in a system of interior drainage; no great waters run to the ocean, only rivulets trickle into desert "sinks," there to seep away and dry. The average annual rainfall is less than eight inches. Barren mountain ranges and arid plateaus mark the landscape, creating deep valleys spotted by dry washes and the ever-present sagebrush. The natural population consists of rabbits, coyotes, other small mammals, and numerous desert birds and reptiles. There are also more than ninety valleys where agriculture has been carried on with the aid of irrigation and careful husbanding of stream or rain water, in some cases for thousands of years.

This strange territory has acted as a magnet to various sorts of people, affecting them all in some way. The aboriginal inhabitants survived by hunting, gathering, and primitive farming. Among the earliest white explorers were trappers, who enriched themselves by virtually decimating the fur-bearing population of the stream banks. Travelers of the California gold rush period hurried through the area, cursing the heat and aridity of the sunlit land. The ore discoveries on Virginia City's Sun Mountain brought a horde of adventure seekers, town builders, promoters, and—ultimately—state incorporators. The migrants contributed to widespread conceptions about the state and region.

A former president of the United States, according to popular rumor, designated the Comstock mines "as close to Hell" as he cared to go. Yet mining was exceedingly important. Hundreds of legends arose from dreams of fortune and a few realizations of bonanza: a drunken prospector fell and broke his whiskey bottle on what proved to be a rich piece of ore; a runaway burro kicked open a fabulous lode; a miner answering nature's call uncovered a vein that made him wealthy. Historians have asserted that the output of Nevada's mines and the desire to have new money for the Union cause in the Civil War brought statehood, a notion that ignores both the fact of minimal Copperhead activity and the further fact that the bullion could have been obtained for the Union cause anyway. Nonetheless, the time was colorful if somewhat economically and socially erratic. The Tonopah-Goldfield discoveries nearly a quarter of a century after the Comstock's decline brought a period relatively more stable but similar to the earlier era and, inevitably, the "bust." Despite the shortness of these mining cycles, Nevada has often been declared a mining state nearly without qualification.

Then, there were lawyers. Nevada was considered a lawyer's utopia from its earliest days. The complexities of interpreting a mining law giving a claimant the right to "dips, spurs and angles" of an ore vein made many an attorney more wealthy than the people he served. The existence of sparse water supplies also enriched advocates who helped farmers preserve their "grab" rights to the liquid. In later years, increasingly easy divorce laws brought fortune to new generations of legal advisers.

Very early, there were tourists. Despite Nevada's notorious deserts and undependable economy, the liberal attitudes of citizens toward gambling, prizefighting, and other entertainments contributed to an attractiveness to travelers. These often thought of the state as a vast playground, amusement park, or variety of human zoo.

Through every period came also the writers. Perhaps no other state of the Union has enjoyed so much attention from popular and semischolarly title-givers. Nevada was a "jungle," a "rotten borough," a vast and unexploited archeological "dig," a constitutional aberration, or a veritable paradise of "ghost town" remnants of the effort to build a mining industry. This treatment created among some segments of Nevada society a defensiveness and a type of isolationism that helped to obscure the truth of its participation in western American life.

Despite the indignities suffered at the hands of exploiters and journalists, Nevada was from its inception a part of national movements. The changes and developments that characterized the nation found prominent representation in the Far West. Civil War patriotism in the country prompted ready response within the Great Basin; the arena of politics found audience and players in a western setting; economic depression affected even isolated westerners; during periods of unrest or interludes of peace, the attitudes of Nevadans paralleled those of other Americans. A catalog of problems and grievances, hopes and desires, compiled by citizens of the thirty-sixth state would probably have read very much like that put together by residents of almost any other.

In 1890, the frontier period of the United States was officially declared at an end, and theoretically the western region commenced to mature. To a large extent, Nevada, too, began to come of age during the 1890s—following the Comstock bonanza and before the boom at Tonopah. Because the Comstock was finished, it seemed necessary to reassess the state's resources and needs. The solutions to problems appeared vital to the survival of the state; thus a depression in mining led to the opposite condition in politics. The political movements then current in the nation found not only response in the West, but even exaggeration. Because the population was small, single figures appeared larger than ordinary. Trends only moderately significant elsewhere were magnified in Nevada almost into life style. Institutions constructed as temporary measures became permanent, inflexible, and conventional, affecting generations who would not be vouchsafed an opportunity to undo tradition. Nevada's lot was decided then: victim of exploitation for private gain, prey of writers and journalists, martyr to manipulation, sufferer from social ostracism, yet all the while attractive to those who believed it might be otherwise.

I

The National Background of the "Silver Crime"

NEVADA entered the Union "battle born," a host to miners, and largely Republican in politics. The early years of the Comstock lode had brought the territorial region nearly enough real and prospective population to suggest that statehood might be attained in the near future. Meanwhile, a Republican president realized that conditions surrounding the nearly ended Civil War would demand astute political measures. Abraham Lincoln sponsored statehood for Nevada and appointed Republicans to key positions in the interim before state elections took place, thereby assuring two Republican senators to vote for his Reconstruction proposals. The aftermath of this series of events set the political tone for the new state during the next quarter century. With the single exception of James G. Fair, who served only one term, all of the state's United States sena-

tors before 1892 were Republicans; four of the six governors were Republican; eight of ten congressmen were
Republicans; the legislature was also dominated by that
party. In short, the Grand Old Party nominally controlled
the infant state's electorate. Nevertheless, beginning as
early as 1873, national and local events combined to reverse
the political trends in the new commonwealth. Nevada
would greet the twentieth century leaning to the left in
political philosophy, nearly devoid of miners, and pre-
dominantly Democratic. Perhaps no other western state
underwent so dramatic a change during the last quarter of
the nineteenth century. The causes for these phenomena lie
in the so-called Crime of '73.

The drama began unexcitingly in 1871, as the United
States Congress began to consider an "omnibus" mint bill,
setting forth standards of coinage and regulations for the
manufacture of the nation's money. The proposed act,
sponsored by Senator John Sherman of Ohio and discussed
in the House and Senate for more than two years, was
ostensibly designed to bring up to date the standard for
United States coinage. Until the 1870s, the currency of the
country was a rather casual item, with the coins of other
nations as well as those of the United States freely circulating and readily accepted as legal tender. As the nation
emerged from the Civil War with unification at all levels
as a goal, a need was felt to bring better coherence to the
money system.

Few people understood the operation or the philosophy
of the monetary system, and explanations were rarely simple
enough for easy comprehension. The relationship between
the circulating medium, the prices of various goods and
services, and the government's role in regulating the econ-

omy were all involved. Most businessmen and investors adhered to the so-called bullion theory, holding that the value of money was determined by its bullion backing, or security. A coin was a token or symbol of a set amount of bullion. Adherents of the bullion theory believed that any government interference with the value of bullion was unsound. Therefore, the government's function was to issue only that money—coins or currency—secured by bullion in government vaults. While the market value of gold and silver was reasonably stable, bullion theorists accepted the form of bimetallism that meant coinage of gold and silver at some fixed ratio (15.999 ounces of silver to 1 of gold, for example). When the prices fluctuated, however, orthodoxy demanded a single gold standard.

At about the time the mint bill was under discussion, ideas about the system were undergoing a change. Money and credit, rather than money and bullion, were thought to be interconnected. Furthermore, the government was allotted a more active part in regulating the monetary system under the new theory. Adherents to the money-credit philosophy pointed out that gold as security for circulating currency made the system inflexible in a time of expanding business activity; the money and credit supply should be capable of expanding whenever necessary, for the sake of both business and the public. These easier-money ideas found favor with agrarian groups of the South and West and with debtors everywhere; they were in the background of arguments over the system of coinage.

The western states and territories had a considerable stake in the American coinage system, for it was in the West that a major part of the nation's precious metals—the raw material of coins—was mined. The industry was particularly important in Nevada: the Comstock lode began to boom in the 1870s under the influence of the "bonanza kings." Silver and gold poured from western rocks. Under the circumstances, the western senators might have been expected to take an active role in the debate on the mint bill.

When the proposed act appeared on December 16, 1872, Senator Sherman spoke in its support and led the discussion on amendments. The Senate Committee on Finance, of which Sherman was the chairman, now proposed minor modifications in a single section of the bill.[1] Nevada's senators sat silently in the chamber during the session.

Not so complacent was the editor of Virginia City's *Territorial Enterprise*. Writing from his office directly over the Comstock lode, he found the proposed act a danger to the nation's economy. Pointing out that Sherman's bill proposed to depreciate the value of the silver in circulating coins, the editor associated the falling price of silver with the price of gold. He suggested restoring silver to a broader circulation, saying that the mint bill, if passed, would drive silver out of circulation in the country. Expanding his argument, the scribe declared:

We do not exactly understand . . . Senator Sherman's bill. . . . The bill provides for a trade silver dollar of . . . 440 grains troy. . . . The weight of the American silver dollar now is 412½ grains, while the half dollar is but 192. The dollar is therefore worth, intrinsically, 4½ per cent more than the half dollar, which virtually excludes the former from circulation.

The editor continued, reviewing the historical position of the coins, and pointing out that with the increase in the silver supply (and the consequent drop in its price), the price of gold was rising. He suggested increasing the coinage of silver, not decreasing it, as he said the Sherman bill would do.

The restoration of silver to circulation amongst us would be likely to check a decline which was caused principally by the practically simultaneous withdrawal of the metal from the currency of France, the United States, and Germany. In our estimation, Mr. Sherman's bill commences at the wrong end of the difficulty. We are tending yearly toward the resumption of specie payment, and to save our silver coinage from further depreciation, it should be substituted for the paper fractional currency now in almost exclusive use in the Eastern States.[2]

This editorial showed an awareness of several national trends which were linked to the coinage problem. The end of the Civil War was the beginning of a period of widespread discontent. A major problem was the fluctuation and disequilibrium in the money supply. This economic confusion was blamed on a number of special capitalistic interests. Railroad companies exploited their customers through outrageous fees; industrial monopolies held up prices and raked in huge profits; and the national banks charged ruinous interest rates. Wartime inflation had brought inevitable deflation, and people began to feel that their former confidence in the ability of big business to maintain prosperity had been misplaced. From 1865 to 1870, money in circulation dropped from $31.18 per capita to $20.10. At the same time, the general base-price index fell from 132 to 87, and farm prices declined even more rapidly.[3] The response to these varied pressures was the inauguration of the Granger movement, begun in 1867 as the Patrons of Husbandry.

The Grangers, under a variety of names, entered politics

with demands for restrictions on monopolies and industries and for reform of the currency. When the Grangers' influence declined in the 1870s, after failure to bring about the desired reforms, their platform was mounted by the Greenbackers. The Greenback party offered its first national candidates in 1876 and polled about a million votes in the congressional elections of 1878. The Greenback movement, also begun in the 1860s, was devoted largely to demands for expansion of the currency and more liberal issuance of paper money. The normal working of the monetary system caused money to be plentiful in good times, thus allowing widespread speculation, and scarce in hard times when more circulating medium might have restored sagging markets. This, combined with government policies that generally favored dealers in hard money, spurred not only Greenbackers but many others to believe in inflation. There was, throughout the period, a continuing feeling that the needed expansion could come from a freer coinage of silver.[4]

Alternatives to such expansion were offered as well. Opponents of free silver recognized the need for reform of the nation's monetary system, but pinned their hopes on the gold standard or similar schemes. One such proposal was that bank notes should be backed by the assets of national banks; others suggested that reserves against bank deposits should be maintained at greater or lesser levels in an early version of the idea of a "managed currency." Silverites recognized that such plans might have a further deflating effect, and some silver men supported inflational proposals to repeal the prohibitively high taxes on state bank notes.[5]

The silver issue was, of course, more than just a money problem. It became a symbol to disparate segments of the society. Expansion of the currency meant to farmers that they could hope to be freed from constantly increasing burdens of industrialism. Labor came to believe that free silver might somehow aid in the fight to end injunctions against strikes, or help to equalize the tax burden. Gold-standard men grew to think that free silver would disturb the economic—ultimately the social—status quo, leading the nation to anarchy and financial chaos.[6]

Sherman, meanwhile, continued to press the mint bill through Congress. The bill returned to the Senate on January 7, 1873. After brief discussion, the proposed act was again ordered printed in full with further amendments.[7] On January 17, the senators met as a committee of the whole. At this session occurred one of the substitutions that earned the statute the label of the "Crime of '73."

The clerk read the entire bill, with amendments. Senator Sherman defended the proposed act against pointed remarks from Senators Cole and Casserly of California. The major issue was the striking of Section 15, which referred to recoinage of damaged gold pieces. The elimination of the controversial section gained the senators' agreement. The next section, number 17, defining minor coins, became Section 16 and was adopted with insignificant changes. The action, however, confused the numbering, giving later speech-makers a point to argue. Section 17 (formerly 18) contained no disputed points and was adopted without comment. The discussion turned next to Section 19, which then became 18. This described the devices to be engraved on "the gold dollar and three-dollar piece, the silver dollar, half dollar, quarter dollar, the dime, five, three, and one-cent piece." Again the California senators entered the discussion, challenging Sherman for explanations, which he

gave calmly. Nevada's senators indicated only casual interest in the proceedings. Senator Eugene Casserly of California was the only person who showed any concern with
problems of silver, when he remarked during the argument
over charges for coinage, "We have more silver than we
want. Nevada appears to be getting ready to deluge the
world with silver." Casserly suggested that the falling price
of silver might make it a good medium of international
exchange.[8] This, despite the fact that most European nations
were then abandoning the white metal in favor of gold for
settlement of international obligations! Finally, the bill with
amendments was read again to the committee and passed
without a recording of the vote.

When the proposal reached the House of Representatives,
Samuel Hooper of Massachusetts, whose name the document bore, requested nonconcurrence with the Senate-
passed version. Reprinting of the proposed act was ordered
to forestall immediate nonconcurrence. At this time, the
bill was called a codification of existing laws on mints,
assay offices, and coinage.[9] Two days later, Hooper again
asked nonconcurrence and requested a conference. Hooper,
William L. Stoughton of Michigan, and Thompson W. Mc-
Neely of Illinois met with Senators Sherman, John Scott
of Pennsylvania, and Thomas F. Bayard of Delaware.[10]
This group would put the final touches on the alleged
"Crime of '73."

On February 6, 1873, the managers of the conference
committee reported that they had resolved disagreements
by a series of compromises. In the section giving instructions for coinage of money pieces, the wording was now
". . . on the gold dollar and three-dollar piece, the silver
trade dollar, half dollar, quarter dollar, the dime, five, three,

and one-cent piece the figure of the eagle shall be omitted; and on the reverse of the silver *trade* dollar, the weight and fineness of the coin."[11] Thus the bill as it came from the conference provided for the minting of trade dollars usable in settling small foreign accounts, but not standard dollars— the customary symbol of the unit of account. The Senate concurred in the report without a tally of the vote or a recording of objections.[12] The House also concurred without recording the ballots.[13] The president signed the bill, HR 2934, and so informed the Congress on February 14, 1873.[14]

The so-called silver crime was committed, then, in full view of the men who would shortly begin to claim deception and to damn John Sherman for his role in promoting the act. Almost nobody appears to have considered what had happened to the nation's currency, although some were aware of the consequences even before final passage. Conrad Weigand of Virginia City wrote to the editor of the *Territorial Enterprise* on February 4: ". . . through Senatorial stupidity the amendments passed in the Senate have substituted the trade-dollar for the money-dollar. The practical effect of this will be, besides the possible litigation on contracts of old dates, that the international coinage scheme will be broken, and after March 31 of this year silver bars will have to be understamped two and three-tenths cents per fine ounce as compared with present valuation." Weigand said that the devaluation would be disastrous to Nevada, a "threatening discount on the great staple of our Silver State."[15]

Weigand was perhaps a good prophet, but at that time he was unsuccessful in obtaining much attention for his views. The Comstock's bonanza days might last forever, and who could think of politics with such prospects? There is some evidence, indeed, that the capitalists and major mine owners of the Comstock supported the demonetization to their own profit.[16] The trade dollars, legal briefly for payment of domestic obligations up to five dollars only, were heavier than standard dollars, 420 grains to 412½. The weight provision was made to meet the desire to compete internationally—especially in the Orient—with the Mexican peso. It was never intended that the trade dollars should circulate within the borders of the United States; that provision was deleted in 1874. Trade dollars continued to be minted until 1885.

William Morris Stewart, the senator from Nevada, spent most of the balance of his long political career defending his inattention to what became the "silver question." Stewart had been an ornament to Nevada politics from the earliest days. Born in 1827 in New York State, he received his early education near the family home in Ohio. He studied law at Yale from 1848 to 1850, when the California gold rush caught his imagination. In California, Stewart went prospecting, and after some years of fair returns, he decided to try the profession for which he had been trained. The law led him to politics, and in 1854 he was briefly attorney general of California. He practiced law in Nevada City and Downieville, California, until 1859. Then the Comstock rush took him to the mines of "Washoe." Stewart became one of the most influential figures in Nevada law and politics; indeed, he had virtually no other interests with the exception of his family. He served in several posts and actively campaigned on a number of issues in territorial and early statehood days. When Nevada was admitted to the Union, he was selected with James W. Nye to be a United States senator.[17]

Attacking John Sherman after the commission of the "silver crime," Stewart claimed that Sherman had talked continually about a silver dollar and the provisions for inscribing it, but "when [the bill] became law it was found there was no silver dollar in the bill, the trade dollar containing [420] grains taking the place of the silver dollar, and thus silver was demonetized." Stewart further claimed that Sherman "falsified his statements" about the mint bill in debates between the two. He also accused John J. Knox, the comptroller of the currency, of having "got up" the so-called codification, and said, "I have no doubt the scheme was conceived for the sole purpose of clandestinely omitting the silver dollar from the list of coins,"[18] where it had appeared consistently at least from 1836 and sporadically from 1792. Stewart left the Senate in 1875 at the end of his term, returning in 1887. He continued to harass and demean the Ohio senator on all possible occasions after he returned to Nevada politics as well as during the hiatus. The charge was constantly advanced that Sherman deceived his colleagues and plotted to demonetize the white metal.[19] Stewart's defenders and Sherman's detractors often claimed that the Ohioan had plotted with the gold barons of Europe to hold up the price of the yellow metal by demonetizing the white.[20]

Sherman willingly defended himself against the charges of Stewart and his coterie. The Ohio senator declared in his memoirs that the silver dollar was practically an unknown coin by the time the mint bill of 1873 was presented. The first draft of the act, proposed by the secretary of the Treasury, George S. Boutwell, did not include silver dollars on the list of coins. Furthermore, Sherman wrote, reports from various financial experts also favored omitting the silver dollar as a standard unit of money and substituting a gold dollar. Since the silver dollar was apparently passing out of use in domestic circulation, some people—even those who handled fairly large amounts of money—never saw a silver dollar. And, as the codification of the mint laws advanced, Sherman said, "No one proposed to reissue it."[21] To Stewart's charges of secrecy, Sherman replied: "There never was a bill proposed in the Congress of the United States which was so publicly and openly presented and agitated. I know of no bill in my experience which was printed, as this was, thirteen times, in order to invite attention to it. I know no bill which was freer from any immoral or wrong influence than this act of 1873."[22]

The truth probably lies somewhere between these extreme statements. Stewart, a true "political animal," presumably came to realize that he had erred in devoting insufficient attention to the problems of the "honest miner" to whom he had appealed in beginning his career. Sherman, on the other hand, was a member of the conference committee, that worked out the "compromise" substituting the trade dollar for the standard coinage, and he was known to be well acquainted with money and coinage questions. He may thus have been to blame for allegations of a huge international plot that came in the years following 1873.

Whatever the truth, the alleged "silver crime" went almost unnoticed for some years. Coinage and the silver question were not alluded to during the Forty-third Congress. According to some observers, even congressional leaders—including James G. Blaine, the Speaker of the

House—apparently were unaware that silver dollars could no longer legally be coined.[23] At any rate, money problems turned on the currency or greenback question for the next few years. Then, in 1878, when Richard Bland and other new leaders became interested and the consequences of hard money policies became more manifest, some agitation began on the question of the white metal.

Richard Parks Bland's interest, seemingly unrelated to his sectional sympathies—he was born in Kentucky and was from 1872 a Democratic congressman from Missouri—stemmed from a few years' residence in Nevada. There he served as an official of Nevada's Carson County, becoming the protégé and associate of William Stewart. An early campaigner for the free coinage of silver, he successfully sponsored the Bland-Allison Act, passed by the Forty-fifth Congress over the president's veto in 1878. For his work, Bland earned the sobriquet, "the father of the silver dollar."[24] The Bland-Allison Act required the government to buy and mint into dollars between two million and four million dollars worth of silver per month.

When the act was under discussion in the Senate, John Percival Jones, Republican of Nevada, made a major speech. The dissertation took the attention of the senators for several days and, when printed, became a compendium of arguments on the silver question. For this effort, Jones came to be known as the "silver senator," although, having "exhausted the subject," he seldom mentioned the metal again until 1893.[25] Despite these labors and the Treasury's adherence to the minimum standards of the Bland-Allison Act, the demand for silver dollars did not increase and the question was seldom of real concern in national political circles.

Although the great outcry on the silver question was still in the future, because of recurrent hard times, agrarian discontent, and a decline in the silver supply, the problem threaded through political discussions. This is reflected in platforms adopted by national political parties during the late 1870s and 1880s. The Democrats, the Independent (Greenback) party, and the Prohibition party all demanded financial reform in 1876. Only the Prohibitionists mentioned redeeming currency in gold *and* silver in their platform statement. In 1880, only the Democrats discussed the coinage problem in their platform, demanding "honest money consisting of gold and silver, and paper convertible into coin on demand." Reflecting the rising agitation, in 1884 three of the six national political parties inserted into their platforms planks considering the money question. The Democrats announced a belief in "honest money, the gold and silver coinage of the Constitution, and a circulating medium convertible into such money without loss." The Greenbackers claimed to have "forced the remonetization of the silver dollar." The Republican money plank called for "the establishment of an international standard which shall fix for all the relative value of gold and silver coinage." In 1888, the Democrats, despite their early interest and Bland's membership in their party, did not mention coinage in their platform. A reason for this lies in the Republican statement, "The Republican party is in favor of the use of both gold and silver as money, and condemns the policy of the Democratic [Cleveland] Administration in its efforts to demonetize silver."[26] The actions of Republicans Grant, Hayes, Sherman, and others were forgotten in the interest of political expediency that year.

Behind this continuing attention to money problems was

not only the so-called silver question, but also the financial arrangements for the Civil War. In underwriting the costs of the struggle, the national government had issued hundreds of millions of dollars in paper money—greenbacks—unsecured by anything but the government's promise to redeem them at some future time. For a variety of reasons, chiefly lack of public confidence in the government's ability to redeem the notes in gold, the paper depreciated in value and became involved in speculation. Nonetheless, this temporary expansion of the currency offered a pattern for future financial schemes. After the war, however, the notes were redeemed in specie (gold) and retired, causing a contraction of the money supply which furthered the deflationary spiral. Thus, arguments for making both scarce gold and plentiful silver legal tender essentially turned on the desirability of increasing the money supply. The cries for "free silver" or "free coinage," then, actually meant that proponents wanted an expanded or inflated economy; except in rather simplistic terms, "free silver" was not a genuine definition of the desired coinage system, but a slogan or shibboleth serving to rally supporters of easier money. And the "Crime of '73" served to symbolize the complaints about the economic system.

In November, 1889, the National Silver Convention was organized at St. Louis. This organization, forerunner of the American Bimetallic League, adopted resolutions demanding the free coinage of silver and supporting "some friend of silver for the Speakership." William Stewart addressed the convention in a rousing speech, declaring that unless free coinage were attained, civilzation would be "blotted out."[27] The National Silver Convention was active for several years, and had some success in propagandizing the silver cause.

Leaders of the silverites devoted great energy to the proposition of free coinage. In a typical activity, Francis G. Newlands wrote and published a letter to Secretary of the Treasury William Windom, asserting that the act of 1873 was "stupid" and "criminal." Newlands reminded the secretary that his own Republican party was on record favoring bimetallism in the platform of 1888. In refusing to enact laws calling for more silver coinage, the Republicans were violating their own solemn pledges to the people, he wrote.[28]

Several bills for increased silver coinage or larger government purchases of bullion appeared in the 1890 session of Congress. Leading the fight were Senators Stewart and Jones of Nevada and Henry M. Teller of Colorado. President Harrison announced that he would sign no bills providing for free coinage, nor any measure for remonetization.[29] Thus the Republican senators who led the silver forces and the Democratic congressmen who shared their views were unable to cooperate, knowing that the president would veto their efforts. This situation was to continue until the silver question died. However, John Sherman again sponsored a silver bill in 1890. In the famous "log-rolling" session of 1890, easterners and westerners, in order to further their special interests, exchanged votes on a number of issues. Sherman guided to passage a bill calling for the Treasury to purchase four and one-half million ounces of silver each month, with treasury notes to be issued for the market value of the silver bullion, redeemable in either gold or silver coin. The act, which superseded the Bland-Allison Act, did not specifically require the minting of dollars and certainly did not fully satisfy the advocates of free silver. Nevertheless, in return for this action, westerners voted for eastern-supported tariff and antitrust legislation. Despite the maneuver, the amount of money in circulation did not increase and the price of silver continued to be depressed. Dollars continued to be minted until after the turn of the century, about 570 million resulting from the Bland-Allison Act and purchases under the Sherman Act of 1890.

Throughout 1891, supporters of free coinage continued to press their views, hoping to rally enough advocates to force the president to change his mind. At the National Mining Congress in Denver, former congressman George W. Cassidy spoke for the people of his state, saying that "every man, woman, and child in Nevada" was united on the silver question. Cassidy demanded that national political parties be forced to make silver the "dominant issue in the next campaign."[30] Mary Lease, the famous Populist orator, campaigning in the name of the Farmers' Alliance, demanded that the fight against the supporters of the gold standard extend "from the banks of Wall Street to the gates of Hell."[31]

The continuing agitation demonstrated the need for unified action, and the American Bimetallic League was formally organized in Washington, D.C., in May, 1892. Modeled after the "silver clubs," which supporters of the white metal had organized in Colorado, Idaho, Montana, and Nevada, the League pledged in this presidential election year, "We will not support for a legislative or executive office any candidate who is not thoroughly committed by platform and declaration to the full restoration of that monetary system violently disturbed by the legislation demonetizing silver in 1873."[32]

In the face of the declaration, major political parties were forced to act. At their national convention in 1892, the Democrats saluted the Sherman Silver Purchase Act of 1890 with a plank in their platform: "We denounce the Republican legislation known as the Sherman Act of 1890 as a cowardly makeshift, fraught with possibilities of danger in the future, which should make all of its supporters, as well as its author, anxious for its speedy repeal." The Republicans demanded "the use of both gold and silver as standard money, with such restrictions and under such provisions . . . as will secure the maintainance of the parity of values of the two metals."[33]

In July, shortly following the national party conventions, the National Mining Congress allied itself even more firmly with silver. At its national assembly, the Mining Congress enthusiastically adopted resolutions pledging members to vote only for presidential electors devoted to free silver.[34]

This additional support to the silverite forces was attributable to lack of confidence in the major political parties, for despite their platform declarations, it was clear that both Republicans and Democrats were insincere. The Republicans nominated Benjamin Harrison, who had already put his views on the record, while the Democrats nominated Grover Cleveland, a staunch supporter of "sound money" (a euphemism for the gold standard). The people of the West and South who had advocated free coinage of silver now had no home in either of the major parties, so they turned to the Populists, who were unequivocal in their adherence to the cause.

The People's party held an exciting convention in St.

Louis that year. The platform, containing the historic demand for "free and unlimited coinage of gold and silver at the . . . ratio of 16 to 1" was read to uproarious delegates. The scene was compared to a revival meeting; gospel hymns alternated with patriotic songs. The Nevada delegation led the cheer for the money plank in the platform.[35]

When all the conventions were finished, the politicians prepared to travel the usual campaign trail. Often this involved difficult decisions. One of the leaders of the early silver fight, Henry Teller of Colorado, defected to the Republicans. Although an originator of the "Colorado idea" of forming "silver clubs," and a constant supporter of free coinage, Teller decided in 1892 to stay with his party. Much to the disgust of the silverites, Teller endorsed Harrison and urged his followers to support the president. Outraged, the silverite press drew out all the epithets usually reserved for criminals and lower forms of humanity. Teller was a prostitute of the mind and spirit, a tool of the millionaires who had gained control of his party, a treacherous scoundrel and a hypocrite.[36] Hooting and booing silver supporters in Teller's home state of Colorado forced the senator to abandon giving a speech at their convention.[37]

The election season of 1892 was a turning point in western political history. For the next decade, the partisans of free silver became radicals in their cause, allying themselves with other radicals as well. Politicians who had never thought about the evils of capitalism became free-swinging populists; men who had seldom considered money except as a medium of exchange or a unit of account became experts on the complexities of coinage; people who had regarded politics as neither avocation nor career became dedicated campaigners; and advocates who would hardly have expected their divergent causes to be joined discovered that free silver could be political cement. Everywhere in the western mining regions, the excitement was intense and the scenes colorful. In perhaps no other area was this ferment so evident as in the youthful state of Nevada.

NOTES

[1] *Congressional Globe,* 42nd Cong., 3rd sess., Part I, p. 203.

[2] *Territorial Enterprise* (Virginia City, Nevada), December 18, 1872, p. 2.

[3] Fred A. Shannon, *The Farmer's Last Frontier* [Vol. 5 of *The Economic History of the United States* (New York: Rinehart and Company, 1945)], p. 184.

[4] *Ibid.,* pp. 314–315. The standard works on grangerism and the People's party are: Solon Justus Buck, *The Agrarian Crusade: A Chronicle of the Farmer in Politics* (New Haven: Yale University Press, 1920); and John Donald Hicks, *The Populist Revolt: A History of the Farmer's Alliance and the People's Party* (Minneapolis: University of Minnesota Press, 1931).

[5] Milton Friedman and Anna Jacobson Schwartz, *A Monetary History of the United States, 1867–1960* (Princeton: Princeton University Press, 1963), pp. 117–118.

[6] J. Rogers Hollingsworth, *The Whirligig of Politics; The Democracy of Cleveland and Bryan* (Chicago: University of Chicago Press, 1963), p. 34.

[7] *Congressional Globe,* 42nd Cong., 3rd sess., Part I, p. 363.

[8] *Ibid.,* Part II, pp. 668–674.

[9] *Ibid.,* p. 743.

[10] *Ibid.,* pp. 815, 860, 871.

[11] *Ibid.,* pp. 673, 1150. My italics.

[12] *Ibid.,* p. 1150.

[13] *Ibid.,* p. 1189.

[14] *Ibid.,* p. 1364.

[15] *Territorial Enterprise,* February 4, 1873, p. 2. Weigand was an assayer and publisher on the Comstock.

[16] For a discussion of profits to the mine owners and capitalists following the demonetization, see Allen Weinstein, "The Bonanza King Myth: Western Mine Owners and the Remonetization of

Silver," *Business History Review,* XLII, no. 2, (Summer, 1968), 195–218. There was also some profit to local industry, for the CC Mint at Carson City manufactured the trade dollars from 1873 to 1878.

[17] Effie Mona Mack, "William Morris Stewart, 1827–1909," *Nevada Historical Society Quarterly,* VII, no. 1–2, (1964).

[18] William Morris Stewart, *Reminiscences of Senator William M. Stewart of Nevada* (New York: The Neale Publishing Company, 1908, edited by George Rothwell Brown), p. 288.

[19] *Ibid.,* p. 290.

[20] See, for example, Effie M. Mack, "William Morris Stewart, 1827–1909," pp. 61–62.

[21] John Sherman, *John Sherman's Recollections of Forty Years in the House, Senate, and Cabinet* (Chicago: The Werner Company, 1895, popular edition), pp. 391–393. For a recent evaluation of the conspiracy theory of the "Crime of '73," see Allen Weinstein, "Was There a 'Crime of 1873'?" *Journal of American History,* LIV, no. 2, (September, 1967), 307–326.

[22] Sherman, p. 395.

[23] William Vincent Byars, ed., *An American Commoner: The Life and Times of Richard Parks Bland* (Columbus, Missouri: E. W. Stephens, 1900), p. 104.

[24] Myron Angel, ed., *History of Nevada* (Berkeley: Howell-North Books, 1958, photo reprint of 1881 edition by Thompson and West), p. 73; Byars, pp. 36–37.

[25] *Silver State* (Winnemucca, Nevada), May 15, 1890, p. 2.

[26] Kirk H. Porter and Donald Bruce Johnson, comps., *National Party Platforms, 1840–1956* (Urbana: University of Illinois Press, 1956), pp. 53–83.

[27] *Morning Appeal* (Carson City, Nevada), November 28, November 30, December 1, 1889.

[28] *Silver State,* May 24, 1890, p. 2.

[29] *Ibid.,* May 21, 1890, p. 2.

[30] *Morning Appeal,* November 21, 1891, p. 3.

[31] *Ibid.,* March 5, 1891, p. 2.

[32] *Ibid.,* June 4, 1892, p. 2.

[33] Porter and Johnson, pp. 86–93.

[34] *Helena (Montana) Independent,* July 16, 1892, p. 1.

[35] *Silver State,* July 8, 1892, p. 3.

[36] *Ibid.,* September 21, 1892, p. 2.

[37] *Ibid.,* August 1, 1892, p. 2.

II

Background of the Silver
Question in Nevada

In 1890, Nevada contained fourteen counties. The major
towns were the old mining camps of the Comstock and the
east-central district of Eureka, and the little cities along
the Central Pacific–Southern Pacific railroad (mainly Reno,
Winnemucca, and Elko). Carson City, the state capital,
was neither mining camp nor railroad terminus, being
served only by wagon road and the narrow-gauge Virginia
and Truckee railroad. Reno, the largest city and main railroad and trading center, had a population of about 3,500.

Politically, the state was dominated in the early 1890s
by the men of the Comstock, who—even though the great
silver veins played out about 1880—still claimed the right
to move the levers of political power. The eastern part of
the state, where the White Pine and Eureka mining rushes
had created excitement from the 1860s, was also important.

The Comstockers might dominate, but the eastern county citizens within the parties also had to be satisfied. Overlying and underlying this superficial power structure was the force of the railroads. As in many other states, the representatives of these corporations claimed a number of political privileges from their nominal customers. They dictated choices of candidates, decided who might be elected, and when occasion demanded, bought the franchise of elector or elected. When the legislature met, it also was subject to the fiat of the railroad companies on any problem that might affect the business of the corporation. The railroads were especially attentive to their need to retain their own men in the United States Senate. This was a major concern. A county assessor or treasurer, a legislator or other minor official might be influenced when the time came, but to control a United States senator constantly was an absolute necessity.

Particularly important in the political process were the state's newspapers. The publishers or editors, persons of stature in every locality, were generally well educated for the time and devoted to increasing knowledge among their readers. However, each editor or publisher was—and was expected to be—decidedly partisan in his outlook. The coverage of both national and local news was generally fairly good, if somewhat limited by space in four-page papers that gave two pages or more to advertising. In the allotted columns, some papers printed accounts of the proceedings of political, legislative, and judicial bodies, often with more detail and forthrightness than did the official reports. Every newspaper in the state was influential in the politics of the region, and therefore the politicians were careful to maintain good relationships with the scribes.

The practice of politics required that prospective candidates receive nominations from county or state conventions. In a presidential year, the state party chieftains met in the spring in order to select delegates to the national conventions. In all election years, the regular state conventions met in late spring or midsummer. Delegates to state and county conventions were chosen part of the time by "primary elections," part of the time by the central committees (executive boards) of the parties. Between conventions and elections, the central committees conducted the business of the parties. The electorate never numbered more than about twelve thousand during the 1890s; thus an enterprising politician could become acquainted with virtually every voter.

The politicians themselves were produced by the times and the environment. Because of the economic difficulties stemming from the decline of mining, people who could afford to leave Nevada went to other states and only those persons stayed who were well established or too poor to go. The resulting dull times made politics as an avocation an outlet for men seeking either power or associations. While some may have been motivated by a sincere idealism, more apparent was the desire to seize opportunities presented to attain the status of leadership or preferment, however small the milieu. Nor were such attitudes unique to Nevada. The last quarter of the nineteenth century was marked in many states by politics for the sake of power and patronage. The idealist, reformer, or promoter of principle was an oddity. Men who entered politics, then, often did so to fulfill their needs in the fashion of the era—from an election stump or in privileged councils.[1]

In the winter of 1884–1885, the silver question became particularly acute in Nevada. It had long been evident that the glory of the Comstock and the eastern mines would be no more, although no patriotic Nevadan—in or out of politics—would dare to say so. The population had declined with the economy. From 1880, at the beginning of the depression, to 1890, the number of inhabitants slipped from 62,266 to 47,355; almost a quarter of the population left the state during the decade. Another 10 percent were to leave in the next ten years.[2] The state's plight was first blamed only in part on the demonetization of silver.

Politicians in the state had recognized some of the difficulties. The passage of the Bland-Allison Act had received a prompt response from Nevada's political parties, both Democrats and Republicans hailing Bland's achievement in their platforms in 1878.[3] With the problems partially solved in 1880, however, neither party mentioned the silver question in the declarations, concentrating instead on national issues in a presidential year.[4] In 1882, both major parties inserted silver planks in their platforms, but the major concern was in demanding relief from the exactions of the Central Pacific railroad.[5] In 1884, both parties strongly condemned the "silver crime," but again sternly censured the Central Pacific for dictatorial policies and outrageous charges.[6] Clearly, the thinking people of the area regarded as the twin causes of their troubles the demonetization of silver and the depredations of the railroad. The corporation allowed the condemnation to stand virtually unchallenged for reasons of its own. Other problems throughout the decade included attempts to make agriculture a paying business. None of the issues offered easy solution, but the silver question was the most obvious to depression-ridden citizens; thus it was to this that they turned.

When the state legislature opened for its regular session

in January, 1885, one of the first orders of business was the introduction of a resolution demanding the free coinage of silver. Also early on the agenda was action on an invitation from a Denver group to the Nevadans to attend meetings of the National Silver Convention in the Colorado city. An appropriation for expenses of three delegates passed the state senate. A week later, a group of senators proposed that instead of financing a delegation to Denver, the money might well be used for a conference in Nevada on the silver question. After discussion, it was decided that a silver conference would be held in the state senate chambers in Carson City on January 31, 1885, with five delegates allowed for each county.[7]

When the convention opened, C. C. Stevenson, a future governor of the state, was elected chairman. Stevenson addressed the delegates, saying that the object of the convention was "to devise some means to relieve the producers of silver of the onerous burdens placed upon that industry." He proposed erecting a permanent organization that would lead to a call for a national convention. Colorado men had already organized such a meeting, Stevenson pointed out. A long paper by one of the delegates, outlining the history of the silver problem, claimed that the East was the enemy of the West on the silver question, largely due to the easterners' ignorance. Following the reasoning of many other westerners, the document charged that the demonetization of the white metal was the result of a worldwide conspiracy of certain international financial interests. Other speeches in the same vein followed.

At the evening session of the convention, the members adopted a constitution and bylaws designating their organization the Nevada Silver Association. The initial documents provided for annual meetings and for qualifications for membership. Finally, the convention adjourned after saluting the efforts of the Colorado silverites and electing an executive group to direct the affairs of the association.[8]

The Silver Association's effort was rewarded as the state's political parties became more militant. In 1886, the first four planks of the Democratic platform denounced the silver crime and demanded free coinage of silver. The Republicans generally agreed. Both parties again requested regulation of the railroads.[9] In the same year, candidates began to make arm-waving speeches deploring the demonetization of Nevada's major product.[10] Newspapers carried romantic or straightforward editorials on the same topic. Typical was a Carson City *Morning Appeal* editorial published in 1889:

The elixir that will restore Nevada to her former youth and freshness is the restoration of silver to par. . . . The great money monopolists in the East . . . are using all their power to destroy the greatest industry in the state. . . . [Restoration of silver would help the state to] show the world that she is entitled to be a State on the grounds of her agricultural industries as well as her mining interests.

Remonetization of silver, wrote editor Sam Davis, would "put new blood into every industry in America."[11]

On November 2, 1889, the *Morning Appeal* carried an important article. With approval, Davis cited a piece from the Winnemucca *Silver State,* which said in part:

The friends of silver must place the interest of the metal above party, or better yet, organize a party whose principal plank shall be free coinage and full remonetization of the metal. Such a party can hold the balance of power in Congress and the next Presidential election if, in the meantime, the old parties do not adopt its principles.[12]

The *Silver State,* through its editor George Nixon, became the leading advocate of free silver in the state, and the powerful spokesman of the party which the editor had proposed. Davis of the *Appeal* was an equally aggressive partisan until near the end of the 1890s. For the time being, however, the editors were ambivalent in their expressions regarding a third-party movement, first favoring, then rejecting such a proposition. Possibly they regarded the threat to form a third party as a political weapon of some stature. Nixon's remark about the proposed new party's holding the balance of power was a significant and recurring theme in the literature of the period.

Meanwhile, the state's politicians tried to work within the traditional framework, although they became progressively more strident in their demands for "justice" to the white metal. The state's newspapers contributed to the ferment by printing large amounts of silverite material. Nationally, a similar furor continued. In November, 1889, a call went out for the National Silver Convention to be held in St. Louis the next year. Although he had approved the proposal of his colleague at Winnemucca for a new silver-oriented party, Sam Davis commented, following the announcement of the St. Louis meeting, that each major party should have "equal representation."[13]

Nevadans began 1890 with hopes for economic revival. A number of prominent businessmen of the western area organized a "Board of Trade," planning to advertise the resources of the region. The leading questions continued to be the dream of remonetization and a desire to spur a profitable agriculture.[14]

In mid-spring, the National Silver Committee suggested that state conventions be held to consider the silver situation. Former congressman Thomas Fitch issued the invitation in an address to the people of his state. According to Fitch's instructions, county residents were to meet in their courthouses on May 24, 1890, to elect delegates to the state convention May 29, in Carson City.[15]

Reaction to Fitch's call for a silver convention was generally favorable. However, while some persons continued to regard the silver issue as essentially nonpartisan, demands for the convention to organize a party also persisted. In Winnemucca, the center of mid-state agitation, a miner proposed in a letter to the *Silver State* that the convention prepare nominations for office and present Thomas Fitch as a candidate for Congress.[16] Fitch, at that time vice-president of the National Silver Committee, and a witty and eloquent orator, was usually in demand as a speaker for the cause. During the spring of 1890, he gave talks on the silver question in the East, Middle West, and South, always to large audiences.[17]

Born in New York State in 1835, Fitch was a pioneer of Nevada. He was a member of the state's constitutional convention, a practicing attorney on the Comstock, and was elected to Congress for a single term in 1868.[18] The former congressman, probably planning a new term in the House for himself within a regular party, ignored the demands for a new partisanship and worked to unite the people of his state on the silver question—within the traditional structure. The silverites of 1890, at least, would be independent of partisan politics, would make no nominations, distribute no spoils. The editor of the *Silver State* wrote that the convention would demand only free coinage: "ask nothing more and accept nothing less."[19]

When the Silver Convention of 1890 met in Carson City, delegates appeared from every county except two. Thomas Fitch made one of the outstanding speeches, spiritedly condemning the silver crime and favoring free coinage. The delegates were nearly unanimous in disclaiming "any connection with politics on the part of the Convention other than as it affects free coinage of silver." Unanimously, the convention passed a resolution instructing the state's congressional delegation to support the cause. Almost in unity, the members resolved that the state's senators and congressman should support no measure that did not require remonetization. Finally, the convention created a central committee, with power to call another convention.[20]

The state's political parties held their biennial conventions shortly after the 1890 Silver Convention. The Republican platform was especially firm in its advocacy of the cause, endorsing free coinage of silver and condemning "the iniquitous interlineated law of 1873."[21] The last was a reference to Senator William Stewart's claim that the confusion created by the substitution of section numbers in the mint bill had allowed the act's managers to insert the demonetization provisions. The Republicans further called the silver crime "an attack on the rights and interests of the miners, farmers, and workers of the land." Nevada's GOP proposed that the state's congressional delegation withhold support from administration and party measures "until the east yields justice to the west" on the silver question.[22] The Republicans took every state office in the fall elections that year, polling over 53 percent of the vote.[23]

Optimism for the silver cause received some encouragement. During the summer, the price of the white metal advanced slightly. At that time, Henry Yerington, the general manager of the Virginia and Truckee railroad and never a real supporter of free silver, wrote to William Stewart, "You have no idea how much the present rise in silver has helped Nevada. New mines are being opened daily and everybody feels that there is a great, big future. . . ."[24] Furthermore, as the congressional session continued, it seemed that the westerners would win their fight through passage of the Sherman Silver Purchase Act and the high McKinley tariff. Governor Colcord expressed similar confidence to the legislature in January, 1891. He told the lawmakers that the almost certain favorable legislation would have a marked effect on the state's lagging economy.[25]

The expectation was short-lived, however, and the outlook for a true free-coinage measure dimmed. The editor of the *Salt Lake Tribune,* a firm supporter of the cause, indicated that unless Congress could be "flooded" with letters and petitions, nothing would be done. The writer recommended that the Farmers Alliance be pressed for help.[26] George Cassidy, editor of the *Eureka Sentinel,* wrote in April that the people of his state should abandon the regular parties and elect an "out and out silver ticket." In commenting on Cassidy's proposal, Davis of the Carson City *Morning Appeal* admitted that a "miners and farmers alliance" ticket would be popular and wrote, "Count us in."[27] Near the end of the year, the good feeling of the previous summer had evaporated. The Comstock towns were dull and virtually deserted. The remaining people were said to be living in poverty; Virginia City was "on the bum."[28]

As 1891 ended, opinion in the state solidified. In reflec-

tion of this unity, the *Appeal* editor affirmed: "The remonetization of silver concerns this State more than any and all
other questions of an economic character now before the
people. It means prosperous times, employment for thousands, and a home market for the products of the farm and
dairy."[29]

By early 1892, widespread agreement was still more evident. Joining the *Appeal,* the *Silver State,* and the *Sentinel*
in promoting the silver cause in the state were the *Austin
Advocate,* the *Nevada State Journal,* the *Reese River
Reveille,* the *Winnemucca Advocate,* the *Pioche Record,*
and the *White Pine News.*[30] Other state papers joined the
crusade as time went on, but the *Reno Evening Gazette*
and the Virginia City *Territorial Enterprise,* after a brief
early interest, became and remained firmly conservative
and Republican. The press generally reflected the opinions
of residents; eastern and central Nevadans were "solid for
silver, regardless of party," while the people of the western
area were inclined to think that the problem of irrigating
the state's arid lands was paramount.[31] With the political
season about to begin, the differences in direction and
emphasis became extremely important.

The silver question would ultimately dominate; it had a
wider appeal than the apparently rural problem of reclamation. Reflecting this, Senator Stewart wrote that the demand
for silver literature was "enormous." The mail, he continued, was "loaded with letters asking for silver documents
to meet the arguments of the gold men," who, he noticed,
were "exceedingly active."[32] To meet the expense of printing and sending the material, Stewart was forced to ask a
number of friends, including W. A. Clark, the Montana
"copper king," for help.[33]

While William Stewart actively supported silver, he nevertheless did not favor the third-party movement then gaining momentum in his state, and he tried vainly to halt its advance. A candidate to succeed himself in the United States Senate, he did not wish to lose the perquisites of the partisan office. He used a friend in Carson City to silence an opposition newspaper through the use of patronage in the Mint.[34] The Senator also wrote that he hoped the agitation for a third party could be quieted, adding, "I do not see how Nevada can . . . support an anti-silver party. I hope the Republican Party will not be that party, and that we can cordially support it."[35]

Stewart had cause to fear the political situation, for it appeared that the Democrats might steal the silver issue from their opposition. Henry Yerington wrote in April: "The Democrats are working up this Silver plank, third party move, etc, and I fear our Repub friends are blindly tumbling into the trap. . . . I think the whole thing will fall flat for our people will soon see that it means a weakening of the Repub party and strength for the Democrats [*sic*]."[36]

A few weeks later, Yerington wrote to Stewart again, still worried about the party's situation. By that time, however, conditions had deteriorated somewhat as concerned the Republicans, and the railroad man's main interest was in retaining the Senator's position: "I have just returned from San Francisco and while there I had a long interview with Mr. [Collis P.] Huntington. Among other things . . . he told me most emphatically he proposed to stand by you throughout the fight. Of course, this won't do to be known on the *outside* and therefor I never mention it." Yerington thought, rather foolishly, that the silver issue was dead.

He regretted that the recent Republican state convention had passed a resolution condemning the national Republican administration's attitude toward silver.[37]

Yerington badly misconstrued the situation. The silver issue was far from dead; indeed, it was only beginning to quicken. In fact, the Silver party of Nevada would emerge before many months elapsed to become one of the strongest and most colorful parties in the western United States.

NOTES

[1] For a discussion of politicians' attitudes and motives during the 1890s, see Paul W. Glad, *The Trumpet Soundeth; William Jennings Bryan and His Democracy, 1896–1912* (Lincoln: University of Nebraska Press, 1960), pp. 62–68.

[2] See Appendix II.

[3] *Silver State,* September 21 and 26, 1878.

[4] *Ibid.,* May 12 and 28, 1880.

[5] *Ibid.,* September 6 and 7, 1882.

[6] *Ibid.,* May 3 and June 11, 1884.

[7] *Morning Appeal,* January 7 to 17, 1885, *passim.*

[8] *Proceedings of the Nevada Silver Convention Held at Carson City, Nevada, Saturday, January 31, 1885* (Published in compliance with Concurrent Resolution No. 20 of the Nevada Legislature, passed February 3, 1885. Carson City, Nevada: J. C. Harlow, State Printer, 1885). See also Appendix III.

[9] *Silver State,* September 14 and 28, 1886.

[10] *Eureka Daily Sentinel,* October and November, 1886, *passim.*

[11] *Morning Appeal,* September 3, 1889, p. 2.

[12] *Ibid.,* November 2, 1889, p. 2.

[13] *Ibid.,* November 9, 1889, p. 2.

[14] *Nevada State Journal* (Reno, Nevada), January, 1890, *passim.*

[15] *Ibid.,* May 8, 1890, p. 3.

[16] *Silver State,* May 17, 1890, p. 3.

[17] *Nevada State Journal,* April 9, 1890, p. 2.

[18] Nevada, Secretary of State, *Political History of Nevada, 1965* (Carson City: State Printing Office, 1965), pp. 85 and 110.

[19] *Silver State,* May 22, 1890, p. 2.

[20] *Ibid.*, May 30 to June 2, 1890; see also *Nevada State Journal,* May 30, 1890, p. 3.

[21] *Ibid.*, June 6, 1890, p. 4.

[22] *Ibid.*, June 7, 1890, p. 2.

[23] Nevada, Secretary of State, *Political History of Nevada, 1965,* p. 183.

[24] Henry M. Yerington to William M. Stewart, June 21, 1890. William M. Stewart papers. Nevada Historical Society, Reno.

[25] *Morning Appeal,* January 21, 1891, p. 1 and p. 3.

[26] *Ibid.*, February 11, 1891, p. 2.

[27] *Ibid.*, April 7, 1891, p. 2.

[28] *Ibid.*, December 13, 1891, p. 2.

[29] *Ibid.*, December 22, 1891, p. 2.

[30] *Ibid.*, February 3, 1892, p. 2.

[31] *Silver State,* April 5, 1892, p. 2.

[32] William M. Stewart to S. T. Hauser, Helena, Montana, February 18, 1892. Stewart papers.

[33] William M. Stewart to W. A. Clark, Butte, Montana; George W. Thatcher, Aspen, Colorado; William F. Herrin, San Francisco, California; and C. S. Thomas, Denver, Colorado; all February 20, 1892. Stewart papers.

[34] William Stewart to S. C. Wright, March 3, 1892. Stewart papers.

[35] William Stewart to Charles C. Wallace, March 3, 1892. Stewart papers.

[36] Henry M. Yerington to William Stewart, April 17, 1892. Stewart papers.

[37] Henry M. Yerington to William Stewart, May 4, 1892. Stewart papers.

III

The Birth of the Silver Party

THROUGHOUT the West in the late winter and spring of 1892, enthusiasm intensified for new political action leading to remonetization of silver. Senator Henry M. Teller of Colorado, then a leader of the cause, was quoted and praised constantly in the western press; his "Colorado idea" for formation of nonpartisan political associations to support free coinage was on lips and pens throughout the region. The "idea" had led by early spring to organization of hundreds of Teller's proposed "silver leagues" or "silver clubs." However, as the political season drew near, it became increasingly evident that third-party sentiment was growing.

One demonstration of western feeling came when a group of Colorado politicians renounced their old affiliation with the silver clubs and commenced to organize politically on a large scale. They were ready, the leaders said, to support candidates of a third national party.[1] Nevertheless, the "silver club" movement continued. In Nevada, at least, the silverites were not yet ready to leave the Republican or Democratic parties.

George Nixon, the well-known editor of the *Silver State,* spurred the organization of the Nevada silver clubs. At the "most earnest and intelligent meeting that ever assembled in Winnemucca," Nevada's first silver club met on April 10, 1892, and elected Nixon the chairman. The organizing resolution demanded a free-coinage man for president of the United States, but the club's leaders still suggested waiting until the national political conventions were finished before the "club" became a "party." The meeting was spirited, but as Nixon wrote wryly afterward, the speeches tended to be one-sided, since "no argument could be had as all thought one way."[2] During the same week in April, 1892, a similar meeting held at Eureka organized an 800-member silver club, and elected Thomas Wren chairman. The Eureka meeting, like others around the state, was described as "large and enthusiastic."[3] This gathering contained one of the most distinguished organizing committees in the state, including two former congressmen, Wren and George Cassidy, and Henry Rives, a judge of the local district court.[4]

In the state capital in the spring of 1892, a few silver men met at the Carson Opera House to form a silver club. Leaders in the capital city were O. H. Grey, the secretary of state, editor Davis of the *Morning Appeal,* Attorney General James Torreyson, Lieutenant Governor Joseph Poujade, and Surveyor General John Edward Jones. In the conservative little western-region city, a mob formed outside the opera house to jeer the silverites. All the state officials except Jones became so frightened by this outbreak that they never again were identified with the silver movement.[5] By 1895, Grey, Torreyson, and Poujade were out of state government, while Jones was the governor and Davis shortly became state controller.

In 1892, Jones was serving his second term as surveyor general of Nevada. Born in Wales in 1840, and taken to the United States as a boy, Jones had lived and worked in many places throughout the West before moving to eastern Nevada in 1869. His main interests were in irrigation and reclamation of arid lands; he was perhaps one of the area's outstanding authorities on these topics, although largely self-taught. Beginning his political career as a Republican, he eventually absorbed many of the ideas of the Populists. A rather reserved and quiet man, Jones seldom made speeches, preferring instead to meet people as individuals and thus gain their confidence.[6]

Meetings in other counties that spring of 1892 were generally of the same stripe as those in Eureka and Winnemucca: noisy, enthusiastic, deadly serious, and often with a revivalistic fervor. A Silver Leaguer at Winnemucca tried to capture the emotionalism of the time in a six-stanza lyric published in the *Silver State,* saying in part:

> The silver leagues are moving,
> You have heard their cheery tone;
> The bugle calls for freedom—
> For our fathers silver coin.

> They are on the track of Sherman
> And his tricky coinage bill
> It robbed millions of our people,
> The bankers vaults to fill.[7]

When the major state parties met in the spring of 1892, each group endorsed the silver cause. The Republicans would later split on the question, but they said early in their platform statement: "We condemn the administration of President Harrison and the action of Eastern Republicans insofar as they have failed to remonetize silver."[8] The Democrats, who hoped that silver men would capture their national convention, passed a significant resolution: "Resolved, that in the event of the Chicago national convention failing to nominate candidates who are unequivocally in favor of free coinage of silver . . . the nominees of this convention are hereby absolved from all obligations to support the nominees of the national Democratic party."[9] The Prohibitionists also joined in demanding remonetization.[10]

The national parties met in June, with the Republicans holding the first convention in Minneapolis. Westerners, though already despairing of hopes for a silverite president, declared their determination to support only a "man who will best serve the interests of the Pacific Coast and stand by the silver proposition."[11] Some silverites threatened to bolt the convention if justice were denied the white metal, an attitude partly attributable to a speech by United States senator John Percival Jones. The senator from Nevada had warned the convention that a third party might ripen in the West unless protection were offered "their chief product."[12]

When the Republican meeting ended, an editor at the Nevada state capital wrote: "Yesterday the gold bugs and office holders named Harrison for a second term. The announcement fell like a pall on this section of the country, where his known hostility to silver has made him odious to Republicans. . . . He was not the choice of the people."

The writer predicted that if the Democrats had "sufficient sense to put up a straight silver candidate on a silver platform," they would win.[13] An Elko editor, expressing the outrage of the silverite press, declared that the Republican record "stinks in the nostrils of the people of Nevada," and accused the GOP of contributing to conditions leading to "deserted mining camps, ruined homes and depopulated States robbed of their constitutional rights."[14]

A poll of Republicans in Carson City revealed their sentiments. Governor Roswell Colcord said mildly that Harrison's was not "the best nomination we could have." Henry Yerington thought that Harrison was "all right." Secretary of State Grey "would have preferred another course," and W. D. Jones of the *Austin Advocate* thought the nomination would almost surely lead to a third-party movement, "if the Democrats nominate Cleveland." Former congressman William Woodburn called the nomination "a wet blanket on the voters of the silver-producing states," while former state senator J. W. Haines of Douglas County declared flatly that Harrison could not carry Nevada's electoral votes.[15] Senator William Stewart, asked what might be expected of the Democrats under the circumstances, declared, "Bah! they will do just the same as the Republicans. Why the gold bugs will spend a million dollars, or two millions, if necessary, to buy up the whole convention."[16] Evan Williams, returned from the convention to which he was a delegate, indicated to a writer from the *Appeal* that the Nevadans had campaigned constantly at the national gathering to gain attention for the silver cause; "But," he concluded, "just imagine three votes in a crowd of over a thousand."[17]

When the Democrats met in Chicago, Grover Cleveland was the obvious choice of the delegates, even before the gavel fell to open the convention. The national platform committee heard the pleas of the westerners for a silver plank, but rejected them. The silverites presented a minority report on the platform, but their motions were shouted down.[18] After Cleveland's nomination, the *Morning Appeal*'s editor commented: "The usurers of the world have carried the day in the United States and secured the nomination of two Presidents, each of which is a tried and trusted representative of their interests. . . . No matter which side elects their man Wall Street is safe for four years more and thus the infamy of '73 will not be righted yet awhile."[19] Nevertheless, the westerners were determined to try.

Even before the national party conventions had finished their work, a call went out to the Nevada silver clubs to meet in Reno. Silver Leaguers knew that no matter who won the nomination, they would have important work to do. After the Minneapolis convention, it was clear that their labors would be all the more troublesome. The executive committee of the state Silver League named June 24, 1892, as the date for a state convention "for the purpose of nominating Three Free Coinage Electors," to discuss the possibility of sending a delegation to the People's party convention at Omaha, to select delegates to the important National Mining Congress at Helena, and to do whatever might "become necessary to perfect a State organization." Thomas Wren and George Nixon were among the prominent politicians who signed the notice.[20]

The Silver Leaguers, increasing their support throughout the state, published, and invited everyone to sign, their oath:

We, the undersigned, solemnly pledge, each to the other, our sacred word of honor, not to vote for or in any way assist any candidate for office who will not pledge himself to use every honorable means to obtain the remonetization of silver, and its free and unlimited coinage, and who will not pledge himself to oppose other candidates who will not pledge the same.[21]

The statement was not taken lightly. Hundreds, then thousands, of men swore to support only silverite politicians. Thus when the Silver League convened, the atmosphere was half religious, half political, and completely serious. At this crisis period, outstanding leaders of the cause in Nevada included Thomas Wren, Charles C. "Black" Wallace, George S. Nixon, and George W. Cassidy.

Thomas Wren was one of the first champions of the silver movement in Nevada. Born in Ohio in 1826, Wren migrated to California as a young man. In 1854 he was county clerk of El Dorado County, California, and thus his interest in politics was assured. He studied law and became an expert in mining litigation, finally attaining recognition as one of the leaders of the Bar on the Pacific Coast. In 1863 Wren succumbed to the excitement offered by the "Reese River mines" of central Nevada, moved to Austin, and opened a practice. The next year, the newcomer was district attorney of Lander County. In 1873, he moved to Eureka, where he continued to combine business and politics. He was elected first to the Nevada state legislature and then to the United States Congress, where he served one term. Wren was nominated for United States senator in the 1881 legislature, but was not elected.[22] A Republican, and sixty-six years old in 1892, he was still extremely popular and was regarded as one of the state's great political leaders.

On the opening day of the Silver convention, Wren gave an interview to a reporter for the *Nevada State Journal*. He declared that the only aim of the convention was to nominate presidential electors. Assuring the reporter that the silver movement was "strictly non-partisan," Wren declared that any attempt to "drag the convention into State politics" would be "promptly suppressed." The aim of the convention, he said, was to demonstrate to the East that the West was strong, united, and sincere in its desire for free silver.[23]

Wren was accompanied at the convention and at the interview by Charles C. Wallace, another pioneer politician. Wallace, usually known as "Black" or "Blackie" to mark his strong Republicanism, was undoubtedly the most powerful political figure in the state. Born in Harrisburg, Pennsylvania, in 1834, he arrived in Nevada early in 1863, residing first at Clifton (which later became Austin), later on the Comstock, and still later at Treasure Hill in White Pine County. In 1873, when the new county of Eureka was organized, Wallace became the county assessor. For nearly thirty years more he made his home in Eureka County, where he held office for twenty years. Wallace knew intimately the politics of, at first, the eastern area of the state, and finally, the entire commonwealth.[24] Magnetic in personality, handsome and distinguished in appearance, Black Wallace began to exercise control over the affairs of the state legislature sometime in the 1880s. At the capital, Wallace conducted "a general lobbying business, wholesale and retail,"[25] finally becoming so influential that the press began to protest. Only half in jest, the *Nevada State Journal* editor wrote during the legislative session of 1891: "If all that is said of . . . Mr. Wallace in directing legislative affairs is true, the taxpayers should by all means engage his services and have him exercise his genius in their interests, instead of going through the farce of electing men every two years. . . ."[26]

In gaining control of Nevada politics, Black Wallace managed to attend nearly all public, semipublic, or private meetings where politics was discussed. Often, though not an official delegate at these sessions, he controlled the deliberations and the selection of officers, usually through the acquiring of proxies. Wallace became the protégé of Collis P. Huntington, president of the Central Pacific railroad, and finally, the paid agent of the corporation in Nevada.[27] As a lobbyist before Nevada's legislative bodies, Wallace was concerned for his railroad client from the beginning of the silver movement; beyond this concern, indeed, he had few personal interests and almost no visible family life. When he became one of the chief organizers of the Silver party, the attentiveness to the railroad interest increased. Later, Wallace assumed almost complete control over the party;[28] at the organizational meeting, however, he seemed to agree with Wren, saying only that the people of the eastern part of the state were virtually unanimous in demanding action on the silver question.[29]

A third important figure at the Silver convention was George Nixon, editor of the Winnemucca *Silver State*. Nixon, born in California in 1860, began his business life in an office of the Central Pacific railroad in northern California. He was later a telegraph operator and station agent for the Carson and Colorado railroad at Belleville and Candelaria, Nevada. He entered the banking business in Reno and subsequently organized the First National Bank at Winnemucca. Nixon was a leader in the Nevada silver movement, an organizer of silver leagues, and an important editor after he bought the *Silver State*. Physically,

Nixon was regarded as unimpressive, but he had a good, quick mind and great powers for organization. A friend assessed Nixon as an able politician, clearheaded, honest, and courageous.[30]

Yet another of the state's leaders attending the convention was George William Cassidy. Born in Kentucky in 1835, he had crossed the plains to California in 1857 in pursuit of gold. During the "White Pine rush" of the 1860s, Cassidy moved to Nevada. He worked at Hamilton as a reporter and then as editor of the *Inland Empire,* moving later to Eureka, where he was editor of the *Eureka Sentinel.* Cassidy was elected twice to the Nevada state legislature from Eureka County and served one session as chief clerk of the assembly. A Democrat, he was nominated four times and elected twice to the United States Congress from his adopted state.[31] He was thus well acquainted with the economic and political problems which beset the region. A man of sparkling wit and a well-known raconteur, Cassidy was to give one of the major orations at the convention.

The Silver convention met in Reno's opera house on June 24, 1892. It was the largest gathering of its kind ever held in Nevada to that time. Twelve counties were represented. At the opening of the meeting, Thomas Wren was elected chairman by acclamation. In taking the chair, Wren made a speech that was almost a prototype for speeches on the silver question at meetings of this sort. He reviewed the history of the silver cause and the various congressional actions, concentrating on the theory that the demonetization was a crime and a conspiracy. Wren, a lifelong Republican, then repudiated his party, promising to devote his energies to the cause of the white metal. He reminded his listeners that the silver movement had begun to attract supporters all over the West—enough, he said, to cause "shaking of dry bones amongst the goldbugs and all the enemies of silver." Calling upon his listeners to forget old party loyalties, he urged them to nominate good candidates who could gain support from people outside the Silver ranks. Addressing himself to the members of the old parties, Wren invited them also to repudiate their former associations, warning, "We do not propose to reward you for good behavior, but, as a party, we say if you do not behave yourselves we have the power to punish, and God help you." The delegates cheered and applauded.

At the close of Wren's oration, the committees were appointed to handle the routine business of the Silver League. Following their reports, the crowd demanded to hear from George W. Cassidy. The former congressman was an accomplished and entertaining orator, a vigorous declaimer in the fashion of the time. He spoke for some minutes, advising his auditors to "repudiate the nominees of the Minneapolis and Chicago conventions and to treat those who advocate their election as enemies of the State." In closing, Cassidy promised: "I will advocate the election of the ticket nominated here today from every stump in the State, and rest assured, gentlemen, that it will be elected next November." Those were Cassidy's last words on a political platform. The exertion of the speech ruptured a blood vessel, and he died within a few hours, thus becoming the first martyr to the cause in Nevada.

Despite their sorrow at losing their friend, the silverites finished the business of the convention in harmonious fashion, passing every resolution unanimously. A three-point platform demanded: first, "the full remonetization of silver and the free and unlimited coinage thereof at the present ratio of sixteen to one"; second, the silverites declared they were "radically and unalterably opposed to the National Republican and Democratic parties on the question of free coinage of silver," and repudiated the nominees of the conventions; and third, the supporters of the white metal pledged to uphold their own nominees for presidential electors, promising to oppose any man "for President or Vice President of the United States who is not unqualifiedly in favor of free coinage. . . ."

Following adoption of the platform, the convention proceeded to nominate the electors "by acclamation amid great cheering." Delegates to the People's party convention at Omaha were also authorized to attend the National Mining Congress as the state's official delegation. When the Silver Leaguers named their central committee, George Nixon was chosen chairman. Then "the convention adjourned to meet at the polls in November."[32]

This convention could have formally organized the Silver party—indeed the group was called the Silver party from the time of the convention—but it did not. Leaders like Wren apparently still hoped that a completely partisan movement could be avoided, provided that the silver men demonstrated their strength at the coming election. Thus the Silver League acted like a party in the naming of delegates to the Populist convention and the selection of presidential electors; the men seemed to feel, however, that they had not indulged in partisan politics.

Certainly the Democrats of Reno were undismayed by the silverite activities in their town. On the evening of the first day of the Silver convention, the Democrats arranged a political rally featuring a huge bonfire and a brass band. A crowd gathered on the plaza to hear endorsements of the nominations of Grover Cleveland and Adlai Stevenson for the highest elective offices in the country.[33]

Following the Silver convention, although Colorado and other western silverites cheered the Nevada effort, comment was not uniformly favorable. The *San Francisco Bulletin* said that drawing silverites from the major parties would result in the election of a "monometallist" and named Grover Cleveland as the probable winner. The *San Francisco Chronicle* called the movement "ill advised." Within the state, one of the leading Reno newspapers carried an opinion that the operation was doomed to fail, since Harrison would certainly be elected.[34] Even devoted partisans of the white metal did not yet believe that the formation of a new party would be wise. Francis G. Newlands, important in the national agitation for free silver, announced that he would be a Republican candidate for Congress. In making this statement, Newlands declared his allegiance to silver, but said that the Silver League was not a real party since its only function was to choose presidential electors; he could thus not be a "Silver party" candidate.

Francis Griffith Newlands was a comparative newcomer to the West. Born in Mississippi in 1848, and educated for the law at Yale University, he went to California to practice his profession. There, in 1874, he married a daughter of former Nevada senator William Sharon and subsequently became the manager of the Sharon properties.[35] He was a delegate in 1884 to the Republican convention in California and made a speech supporting Stephen J. Field for president of the United States.[36] In January, 1889, he established residence in Carson City, Nevada, later moving to Reno for the apparent purpose of seeking political office.[37] Admitting that he would be a candidate, Newlands declared in

1890 that he really did not care which political party he joined; he wished to serve the state, especially to work for better water storage, irrigation and reclamation, increased population, and promotion of diversified industry.[38] There is no evidence to suggest that Newlands was insincere in his declarations. He was that exceptional politician who was willing to observe political practice though he was an idealist with a genuine desire to promote constructive projects. Moreover, this idealism would carry him further in Nevada and national politics than the sometimes cynical maneuverings of his contemporaries. The future congressman, who was unremarkable in stature and had rather sharp features, also customarily wore plaid suits—all attributes that made him a ready target for cartoonists. He ran for a state post for the first time in 1892.

Opposition or no, the Silver Leaguers continued to conduct an extensive campaign. The *Morning Appeal* editor proposed that the People's party nominate William Stewart and Richard P. Bland for president and vice-president, or possibly Stewart and the Populist Thomas Watson of Georgia. Stewart accepted the compliment gracefully, saying that he would be a nominee if the people of his state extended the invitation.[39] It was widely supposed that neither Republicans nor Democrats of Nevada would offer any opposition to whomever the Populists nominated; they were urged by several state politicians to make no nominations for presidential electors—to demonstrate their support for silver.[40]

Stewart, as he continued to do throughout his career, meanwhile introduced a free-coinage measure in the United States Senate. The bill passed the Senate 29 votes to 25. At the state capital, a writer asserted that if the bill passed the House, the Silver League or "Silver party" could "pass out of existence."[41] The bill, like its predecessors and its successors, failed to pass in the lower house. Edward Bellamy, the famous utopian novelist, wrote in an article reprinted in the Winnemucca *Silver State* that this failure had "given a tremendous boom to the third party prospects." He predicted victory for the silverites in the coming election and concluded, "It is good to be alive in these days and have a part in these things."[42]

The failure of Stewart's bill also caused a splintering in the already divided parties in his state. In Esmeralda County, the chairman and secretary of the Democratic county central committee resigned their posts. Declaring that they could no longer adhere to the old allegiance, they pledged their support to "any candidate from presidential electors to constable" who would work for the white metal.[43] The Lander County Republican central committee instructed its delegates to the state convention to cast their votes for the "Silver party" electors, and Douglas County Republicans demanded an oath affirming loyalty to the silver cause for voting in their primary.[44] The Elko County Republicans followed a similar procedure.[45]

Meanwhile, the Silver League delegates attended the Omaha convention and ratified the nominations of James B. Weaver and James G. Field for president and vice-president of the United States. The silver men of Nevada were perhaps as dedicated to their cause as any group in the nation. This devotion did not, however, blind them to the features of populism exemplified in their candidate for president. Many editorials praising Weaver called attention to his proletarian background and emphasized his role in America's "class struggle." The man was portrayed as an ideal American candidate. Born on a farm, he had engaged in "manual toil." He was "a champion of the man who earns his living by the sweat of his face." The contest was pictured as one between the people and plutocracy, between the industrial masses and the favored classes.[46] Although they were little associated with industrialism, or even with the agrarians who breathed life into populism, the westerners allied themselves firmly with these interests.

Candidate Weaver toured the West during the 1892 summer campaign, accompanied in Nevada by George Nixon. Enthusiastic cheering inevitably greeted him at the railroad stations and meeting halls along the way. The most important gathering at which Weaver spoke was in Virginia City. There, on August 7, he and Mrs. Mary Lease, who accompanied the campaign train, addressed a "monster meeting." When the train arrived—carrying the candidate and his wife, Mrs. Lease, and Senator Stewart—bonfires, flags, bunting, and a brass band were all in evidence. Over two thousand people crowded the area in and around Piper's Opera House. General Weaver spoke for an hour and a half. Mrs. Lease, in "a most remarkable effort," gave an hour's oration.[47]

Senator Stewart and candidate Newlands, having assessed the state's political temper, joined the Silver League in Reno the day following the rally in Virginia City.[48]

Earlier in the season, it had been generally agreed that the Republicans and Democrats of the state would make no nominations for presidential electors, but would endorse those already selected by the Silver League. This course would obviously have led to a kind of suicide for the major state parties; nevertheless, loyalty to the silver cause was so deep that most party members thought it worth the price. However, the party leaders thought differently and called for nominating conventions to be held in late summer. Both gatherings were near disasters.

The Republicans met in the courthouse in Reno on August 31. About two-thirds of the delegates were silver men, about one-third, loyal Republicans. The loyal, or straight-out, Republicans offered concessions to the silverites in the interests of party harmony. In return for allowing presidential electors to remain unpledged, they promised that the platform would condemn President Harrison's record and demand free coinage of silver. Thereupon three motions came to the floor: (1) to nominate electors pledged to Benjamin Harrison; (2) to nominate independent, or unpledged, electors; or (3) to nominate electors pledged to the Silver ticket. All three motions were shouted down. Finally, the convention decided to select no electors at all, despite the desires of the party leaders. This also failed to satisfy the straight-outs, who adjourned to the Masonic hall to hold their own convention. There, they proceeded to select nominees and to give their loyalty to the national administration, even though reserving the right to differ with the president on financial questions. Secretary of State Grey, himself a straight-out, promised to certify the electors of this group.

The anti-Harrison Republican convention met the next day and conducted its business. The delegates adopted a platform condemning the national administration. They resolved not to choose electors and to nominate Francis G. Newlands for Congress. Newlands accepted the nomination from the anti-Harrison group in a speech in which he promised to work for free silver.

The straight-outs then also tried to nominate Newlands

for Congress. They appointed a committee to visit the candidate to ascertain his views. When the committee arrived at his home, Newlands was "out driving" and unavailable. Yielding finally to a demand to submit his opinions, Newlands sent a letter to the convention. He thanked the delegates for their friendship, but declined to recognize them as legal representatives of the party. He had already received the nomination for Congress from the "regular" Republicans, he wrote. At last, William Woodburn, who had served three terms in the lower house in the 1870s and 1880s, was nominated by the straight-out group. Woodburn accepted the nomination, declaring that he regarded the fight as one of principle and would do his best to win the election. Thus ended what one editor called "the most unique" political convention ever held in the state.[49]

The Democrats suffered a similar division. The nominating convention refused to name presidential electors pledged either to the Silver candidate or to Grover Cleveland, or to select unpledged electors. The state central committee therefore named the electors of the Democratic party of Nevada. Secretary of State Grey also certified this "regular" slate. Grey's action in thus certifying the antisilver wings of both parties as *regular* led the silverites to their final step.

A second problem raised by Grey ensured the formation of a new party. According to Nevada election law, neither the Silver electors nor any other candidate could appear on the ballot except as nominees of a certified party. The Silver League, therefore, needed to regularize its organization and to seek certification.

In Winnemucca, on September 15, 1892, the state Silver League held its second convention. Music from a brass band entertained the delegates in an Armory Hall profusely decorated with flags, bunting, and flowers. In this setting, the Silver party of Nevada was born. After an opening speech by Thomas Wren recognizing the existence of the party, the convention adopted a platform which condemned both Grover Cleveland and Benjamin Harrison for hostility to silver; recognized Weaver and Field as "the only candidates for President and Vice President who are friends to the use of silver as money"; endorsed Senator Stewart's efforts to obtain remonetization and praised him for his work in behalf of Nevada institutions; proposed the building of a competing railroad in Nevada (a scheme which both major parties also endorsed);[50] and presented the candidacy of Francis G. Newlands for Congress, and others to complete a slate. The delegates approved the platform "amid wild cheering."[51]

When his second term expired in 1875, William Stewart had left the Senate and the state and had returned to California. There he again practiced law, this time in partnership with William F. Herrin, an attorney who represented the Central Pacific railroad interests. In 1886, Stewart returned to Nevada, it is usually said at the behest of the railroad's managers. He was again elected to the United States Senate as a Republican, and served until 1892, when the term was due to expire.[52] Stewart was thus at a crossroads in his political life when he addressed the Silver party of Nevada at Winnemucca that September day in 1892.

The senator was no longer young, but he was robust—a tall, heavy man with a flowing white beard, a powerful voice, and a style of speaking that fascinated his listeners. Stewart addressed the delegates of the Silver convention, denouncing both Cleveland and Harrison and endorsing the

candidacy of Weaver and Field. He closed his long talk
with a promise: "If I go back to the Senate at all it will be
by the Silver Party of Nevada and no other party. . . . I
shall have no party in any county but the Silver Party. With
that party I stand or fall. I am with you, friends, and I rely
on you to stand by me as I have stood by you."

Francis Newlands, the nominee for Congress, was also
an accomplished orator, although not so physically attractive as Stewart. In accepting the favor of the Silver party,
Newlands pointed out that he had already compiled a record
of support for free coinage. He was a member of the National Executive Silver Committee, the National Silver
Convention, the American Bimetallic League, and the
Silver League of Nevada. Explaining the background of
each of the national committees, Newlands again declared
his loyalty to the silver cause. He closed by praising the
Silvermen as "a body of courageous, determined men, con-
stituting a balance of power, who . . . will stand for Silver
as the paramount interest of the mining states."[53]

The new party's financial store consisted of assessments
of fifty cents a month levied on each member, and larger
assessments against the nominees for office. The songs of
the campaign were set to the music of a hymn and a mili-
tary air, and were led or sung at the fall political rallies by
groups called variously the "Comstock Silver Quartette"
or the "Silver Party Glee Club."[54] Quickly drawn petitions
allowed the new Silver party to qualify for a place on the
ballot. As the campaign began, the prospects of the new
party were, as General Weaver had written earlier in the
summer, "grand and inspiring from every part of the field."[55]

The story of the election canvass is quickly told. The
older parties were unable to hold their people, even to the

extent of preventing local groups from endorsing the opposition Silvermen.[56] As election day came, it was obvious that the Silver ticket would sweep the state, and hopes were high that the People's party could hold the balance of power in the electoral college.[57] Although those hopes were disappointed in the national election, the Silver and Populist enticement of Nevada was complete. The Democrats took only 6.48 percent of the tally, and the Republicans took 25.4 percent.[58]

The situation was almost ludicrous in a state that had formerly been firmly Republican. George Nixon wrote a humorous piece in which he suggested colonizing the "gold bugs." Nevada could be divided, he wrote, and a new state formed in the "mountain districts of Ormsby and Douglas counties." (The two small western counties were the only ones the Silver ticket had not captured.) The proposed new state would be small, but ample for colonizing the supporters of the gold standard. If there were objections that those districts were too cold in winter, Nixon continued exuberantly, they were still "not near so severe as the cold these gold bugs are now suffering."[59]

On November 12, the Silvermen rallied at a "grand ratification" of the election in Carson City and formed a procession reported to be a mile long through the streets of the capital. Stewart, Newlands, and Surveyor General Jones, "the only state officer who held silver above party," were the guests of honor of a crowd that filled the Opera House. Fireworks lighted the sky. Stewart spoke first, urging the Silver party to remain firmly in control of state politics and to reform the government. Congressman-elect Newlands made a longer talk, emphasizing the possibility that the Silver party could bring about free coinage by uniting its

efforts with supporters in the West and South. George
Nixon, William E. Sharon, Sam Davis, and others made
speeches in a similar vein. "The wildest cheering" greeted
each speaker.[60] Little analysis came forth at the time concerning what had happened, beyond the recognition that
the Democrats had taken the White House and that silver
would soon become an issue of major national proportions.

Nevada meanwhile had given herself to radicalism. In a
sparsely populated state, a small political party had taken
over the governmental power. The noisy cheering and the
uncritical enthusiasm for an emotional issue had removed
the state, at least temporarily, from any possible relief
by the national government or national parties for its
admittedly serious problems. What major party in power
would extend help to a state that rejected both major parties
in favor of a purely local organization? Nevada needed aid
to reclaim her arid land; she needed help to maintain numerous projects within the state; she apparently needed the
national parties in order just to remain a state (even that
status was under attack). A portent of what could occur
followed almost immediately after the inauguration of the
new national administration. The United States Mint at
Carson City was ordered reduced. Henry Yerington wired
to Senator Stewart: "Today director of mint wired Supt.
Hofer to suspend coinage operation first June. This . . . is
ruinous all round. Our people urge that you stop this if
possible."[61] The recklessness in the state continued un-
abated, however, but not without reason.

George Nixon wrote, following the election of 1892,
"Honest men and pure politics and great principles are in
the saddle in Nevada."[62] He failed, however, to examine
the men, the politics, or the principles of which he was

apparently so proud. It seems unlikely that he was unaware of the background of affairs of recent months because of his early and constant involvement in the third-party movement. Other writers in the years following formation of the Silver party were somewhat more expository, if not always accurate.

Sam Davis of the *Morning Appeal* was one of the first to elucidate. Writing in the *San Francisco Call* in November, 1895, Davis called his piece, "Political Revolution in Nevada." He traced the beginnings of the Silver party to the influence of the state's press. After the publishers had "educated" the public away from support of the Republican "creed" (the high tariff), he wrote, the political bosses threatened the newsmen with extinction. The newspaper editors retaliated by demanding payment for all political advertising in advance, a situation which led the political chieftains to designate the members of the state press association as "a gang of bloodsuckers." One politician was so intemperate as to say that political campaigns would be "better conducted without the assistance of the press."

Hearing of the remarks, the press association men determined to wreck the Republican organization. They bound their members to support no man for office "who was not unequivocally committed to the free coinage of silver." The next step was to campaign for a new political party to symbolize this idea. The press men appointed the most experienced political manipulator in the state to the chore of organizing the party in the eastern part of the state, an activity which gained for the Silver party the reputation of being "Black Wallace's outfit."[63]

Wallace was indeed active in organizing and later managing the party. This "quaintest of the many quaint characters that Nevada . . . produced" was virtually in control of the new party from its start until sometime in 1899. After he died, the *San Francisco Chronicle,* in an unsigned article, said that Wallace's activities in the party were designed to advance the interests of the Central Pacific and Southern Pacific railroads. The Silver party, said the *Chronicle* writer, had been established to divert attention in the state from the peoples' grievances against the railroad. This, declared the scribe, was "one of the keenest political moves ever successfully undertaken."[64]

It is surely true that Nevadans and other westerners had cause to be suspicous of the railroad. Having welcomed the coming of the "iron horse" with uncritical enthusiasm in 1869, they soon found that the corporation often imposed exceedingly unpleasant conditions on affected localities. Discriminatory freight rates which strangled infant industries and held back settlement, interference in local politics, and failure to pay a fair share of state and local taxes all caused the Central Pacific with its smaller subsidiaries to be designated a "dictator," a "vampire," and worse.[65] The accusations against the railroad were not merely the fulminations of disappointed office seekers. Available records show the treatment accorded the roads by county tax assessors, making it clear that these officials were the minions of the transportation interest.[66] Thus if the organization of the Silver party was a plot to draw attention away from the corrupt activities of a large corporation, it was a scheme well founded.

Other reasons advanced for the founding of the party came from the various opposition newspaper editors of the state. Almost invariably, Black Wallace was the villain of their pieces. Wallace was said to have entered the silver movement to procure a "corner" on political offices and power. As the "bell weather" [*sic*] of the Republican political bosses, Wallace handled their manipulations.[67] Since the Republicans already controlled the state before the advent of the Silver party, and as the GOP was ultimately almost destroyed within the state by opposition parties, the latter assertion lacks authority.

In 1895, Roswell K. Colcord, a former Republican governor who turned to the "gold bugs," wrote that the Silver party was organized as a Democratic plot to destroy the state's normal Republicanism. No necessity existed, Colcord said, for a silver party or any other third party in 1892. Colcord reasoned that the Democrats garnered support for their scheme because the Republicans were tired of Senator William Stewart, and wished to retire him and "elect a good Republican resident of the State." The senator grasped the opportunity of combining the Democrats with the balance of the voters who (along with the Democrats) were "anti-railroad, anti-corporation, and anti-progress." Francis G. Newlands, the candidate for Congress, also changed his politics, "knowing the Democrats would willingly accept anything . . . in exchange for office, and believing also that enough Republicans could be hoodwinked. . . ." Colcord contended that this combination gave "the spectacle of two practically non-resident railroad candidates running on an anti-railroad ticket." Then, the former governor said, "the entire management of the campaign was placed in the hands of an employee and paid agent of the S. P. Company." The plan worked so well, Colcord wrote, that the Silvermen continued to elect prorailroad candidates on an antirailroad ticket. If it had not been for the conditions he outlined, Colcord believed, "the State never would have been carried by the Silver party, notwithstanding the silver sentiment." Withdraw the conditions, he said, and the state would be safely Republican again.[68]

Governor Colcord's analysis contained a number of interesting points, but he also made a number of errors. If the Democrats plotted to destroy the Republicans by organizing a third party, they must have been very fine prophets, for initial Democratic injuries from the formation of the Silver party were great. In the days before the Silver party came on the scene, the Democrats could elect some officers or lose state posts by a few hundred votes. After the Silver party was organized, until 1900, only Independents or Populists received fewer votes than Democrats.[69] Colcord's assertions concerning railroad control of the candidates were probably nearer the truth.

These second and third thoughts on the founding of the Silver party were little discussed until some years after the party had established control over the state's political processes. Meanwhile, in promoting that mastery, the silverite press continued to be active. At the end of 1892, the *Silver State* printed a typical Western salute to "Judas Iscariot Sherman:"

John Sherman is an old man—old in crime, old in all things that pertain to avarice, greed, treachery, and ingratitude. As old as he is he will live to see the day when his name will be pronounced in the same breath with Benedict Arnold, J. Wilkes Booth and Charles Guiteau. Despised and hated by those he has betrayed he will go down to his grave like the slinking cur that he is, unhonored and unsung. . . . May his villainous soul burn in hell eternally. . . .[70]

With the same sort of assistance, the Silver era continued. Every state office and most local posts were destined to fall to silverites.

NOTES

[1] *Silver State,* April 1, 1892, pp. 2 and 3.

[2] *Ibid.,* April 11, 1892, p. 3.

[3] *Weekly Sentinel* (Eureka, Nevada), April 16, 1892, p. 2.

[4] *Silver State,* April 18, 1892, p. 3.

[5] *Morning Appeal,* September 7, 1892, p. 2.

[6] *National Cyclopaedia of American Biography* (New York: James T. White and Company, 1909), XI, 201; *Weekly Sentinel,* October 13, 1894, p. 3. See also, Nevada, Surveyor General, *Biennial Reports,* (1887–1895).

[7] *Silver State,* May 23, 1892, p. 3.

[8] *Morning Appeal,* June 22, 1892, p. 3.

[9] *Silver State,* May 26, 1892, p. 3.

[10] *Nevada State Journal,* May 7, 1892, p. 3.

[11] *Morning Appeal,* June 7, 1892, p. 3.

[12] *Ibid.,* June 10, 1892, p. 3.

[13] *Ibid.,* June 11, 1892, p. 2.

[14] *Daily Independent* (Elko, Nevada), September 6, 1892, p. 2.

[15] *Morning Appeal,* June 12, 1892, p. 3.

[16] *Ibid.,* June 16, 1892, p. 3.

[17] *Ibid.,* June 17, 1892, p. 2.

[18] *Ibid.,* June 22 and June 23, 1892, *passim.*

[19] *Ibid.,* June 24, 1892, p. 2.

[20] *Silver State,* June 14, 1892, p. 2.

[21] *Nevada State Journal,* June 19, 1892, p. 2.

[22] Myron Angel, ed., *History of Nevada,* p. 427.

[23] *Nevada State Journal,* June 24, 1892, p. 3.

[24] *Weekly Sentinel,* February 2, 1901, p. 3.

[25] *Nevada State Journal,* March 8, 1891, p. 3.

[26] *Ibid.,* March 21, 1891, p. 2.

[27] *Ibid.,* January 31, 1901, p. 3.

[28] *San Francisco Chronicle,* January 31, 1901, p. 7.

[29] *Nevada State Journal,* June 24, 1892, p. 3.

[30] Francis G. Newlands to William F. Herrin, n.d. [1895?] Fran-

cis G. Newlands papers. Yale University Library, New Haven, Conn.

[31] *Nevada State Journal,* June 25, 1892, p. 2; *Reno Evening Gazette,* June 25, 1892, p. 2.

[32] *Reno Evening Gazette* and *Nevada State Journal,* June 24 to June 28, 1892, *passim.*

[33] *Reno Evening Gazette,* June 24, 1892, p. 2.

[34] *Ibid.,* June 27, 1892, p. 2.

[35] James G. Scrugham, ed., *Nevada,* 3 vols. (Chicago: American Historical Society, 1935), I, 363.

[36] A. Russell Buchanan, *David S. Terry of California: Dueling Judge* (San Marino: The Huntington Library, 1956), pp. 199–200.

[37] *Reno Weekly Gazette and Stockman,* January 3, 1889, p. 4.

[38] *White Pine News* (Ely, Nevada), August 23, 1890, p. 2.

[39] *Morning Appeal,* June 28, 1892, p. 2.

[40] *Ibid.,* June 29, 1892, p. 2.

[41] *Ibid.,* July 2, 1892, pp. 2 and 3.

[42] *Silver State,* July 22, 1892, p. 3.

[43] *Ibid.*

[44] *Genoa Weekly Courier* (Genoa, Nevada), August 19, 1892, pp. 1 and 2.

[45] *Daily Independent,* September 13, 1892, p. 2.

[46] *Silver State,* July 26, 1892, p. 2.

[47] *Ibid.,* August 4 to 8, 1892, *passim.*

[48] *Ibid.,* August 9, 1892, p. 2.

[49] *Ibid.,* September 1 and 2, 1892, *passim.*

[50] It should be noted that the Central Pacific–Southern Pacific corporation allowed the politicians and the parties to *say* anything they pleased about the company and its practices. The important item was that the various congressmen, legislators, and especially senators, *act* correctly when it was time to vote on legislation.

[51] *Silver State,* September 16, 1892, p. 2.

[52] Effie M. Mack, "William Morris Stewart, 1827–1909."

[53] *Silver State,* September 16 and 17, 1892, *passim.*

[54] See song sheets in the Newlands papers.

[55] *Silver State,* July 22, 1892, p. 2.

[56] S. P. Howard, Carlin, Nevada, to Enoch Strother, October 21, 1892. Trenmor Coffin papers, University of Nevada Library. Howard complained that the local Republican committee had endorsed Newlands, and had refused to pay assessments to Republican party coffers.

[57] *Silver State,* November 7, 1892, p. 2.

[58] Nevada, Secretary of State, *Political History of Nevada, 1965,* p. 184.

[59] *Silver State,* November 28, 1892, p. 2.

[60] *Ibid.,* November 14, 1892, p. 3.

[61] Telegram, H. M. Yerington to William Stewart, May 25, 1893. Stewart papers.

[62] *Silver State,* November 10, 1892, p. 2.

[63] *San Francisco Call,* November 3, 1895, p. 17.

[64] *San Francisco Chronicle,* January 31, 1901, p. 7.

[65] M. Angel, ed., *History of Nevada,* pp. 272–290.

[66] Washoe and Humboldt counties were perhaps the most important centers of railroad contact in Nevada. In 1891, the Washoe County assessor needed eight pages in a large register to list the properties of the Central Pacific and to enter an assessed valuation of $1,004,380. This figure included 36,047 acres of patented land assessed at less than $1 per acre ($35,845), and 117,000 acres of unpatented land assessed at 20 cents per acre. At the same time, the lowest assessment on any lot in Reno (a plot on the river front) was $75. Most assessments on unimproved building sites were from $200 to $500. If these were generous-sized lots (one-third of an acre), the patented land of ordinary property holders in Reno was assessed at between $600 and $1,500 per acre; the railroad paid taxes on $1 per acre. The next year, the railroad received a reduction of 15 cents per acre on unpatented land.

In Humboldt County in 1892, the Central Pacific held 510,012 acres of unpatented land assessed at $25,000, and 40,261 acres of patented land assessed at $50,326; or under 5 cents per acre on unpatented land and about $1.25 on patented land. At the same time in the Winnemucca area, cultivated land belonging to private citizens was assessed at $5 per acre, uncultivated land at $1.33. In the same county, schools were forced to close early in 1888 because there was no money to pay the teachers.

See Assessment Books of Washoe and Humboldt counties, 1891, 1892. Nevada State Archives, Carson City, Nevada. The reference to the 1888 school closing is from the *Silver State,* May 19, 1888, p. 2.

[67] *Silver State,* May 2, 1892, p. 2.

[68] *Reno Evening Gazette,* September 5, 1896, p. 3.

The Central Pacific and the Southern Pacific were eventually the same. The Southern Pacific absorbed the Central in 1899, and the company became the Southern Pacific. At that time, the Central was bordering on bankruptcy, in spite of its exorbitant rate schedules. The larger corporation then, with more money poured into its operations, improved some roads, built others, and also purchased some of the smaller companies in Nevada and eastern California. See David F. Myrick, *Railroads of Nevada and Eastern California*, 2 vols. (Berkeley: Howell-North Books, 1963), I, 29–33.

[69] Nevada, Secretary of State, *Political History of Nevada, 1965*, pp. 184–187.

[70] *Silver State*, December 14, 1892, p. 2.

IV

The Silver Party's First Term

THE ELECTION of 1892 was not an election for state officers, and the Republicans remained nominally in power in Nevada. The governor and all other elected state officials were members of the GOP; the state senate was Republican, nine men to six. Several of these were serving the second half of four-year terms. The Silvermen controlled the assembly where the two-year terms had allowed a change. Here, there were five members who had been reelected either as Silvermen or as representatives of their old parties, the balance being Republicans, new Silvermen, and a single Democrat. This arrangement was subject to change at the next election; meanwhile, the business of government continued.

As the time for the biennial opening of the legislature approached, George Nixon reminded his readers that the new party had great responsibilities. The legislators of the Silver party must not allow corrupt politics to mar the session, taxes must be reduced, and state payrolls must be

decreased, he wrote.[1] The last two charges reflected the
continued economic difficulties within the state, where
population declined and agriculture and mining remained
depressed.[2]

A third important problem was the question of reclamation of the state's arid lands. Agitation for some kind of
action leading to construction of irrigation works in the
desert valleys of the West had continued in Nevada and
throughout the region for several years. Representatives
from the dry states had organized the National Irrigation
Congress to press the case for reclamation in state and
national legislative bodies. John Edward Jones was a
leader in the Nevada agitation for cooperative work toward
reclaiming the desert. The surveyor general had tried for a
number of years to gain the attention of the legislature to
the end that the lawmakers might pass constructive legislation. A reclamation act, passed in 1889 and repealed in
1891, failed completely to rectify the situation; an irrigation law designed to bring waters under coherent state management met the same fate. In 1893, Jones's report urged
the legislators to recognize that the water and irrigation
problem was more than merely a local annoyance.[3] An
editor in Reno, surveying the state situation, regretted the
disorganized administration of the area's scarcest commod-
ity and the disinterest of farmers and owners of water rights
in constructive laws.[4]

Governor Roswell Colcord addressed the legislature on
the opening day. In the speech, he remarked upon the
depression in the state and the need to restore prosperity.
The governor thought that recovery lay in the direction of
spurring agricultural production through construction of
irrigation works.[5] In reporting the speech, the *Silver State*

writer called it "great only in length," and criticized Colcord for failing to mention either the silver cause or the needed reduction in state expenses.

As the deliberations began, the most interesting questions concerned political alignments. Even as Colcord spoke, there was still uncertainty about who would organize the upper house, where the Republicans had a nominal majority of three. The question was settled when Republican holdover senators J. R. Williamson of Lander County and A. T. Stearns of Eureka voted with the Silvermen, giving the latter a majority of one. Williamson was rewarded with election as president pro tempore of the senate, and Stearns with the chairmanship of the important judiciary committee.[6]

Early activities in the legislature gave a demonstration of the plans of the Silvermen to effect economies and pursue the silver cause. The first assembly bill repealed the 1889 act that had attempted to establish state control over irrigation waters. The first concurrent resolution in the senate memorialized the Congress not to suspend the current purchase of silver bullion under the Act of 1890 (the Sherman Silver Purchase Act). An early resolution in the assembly invited cooperation from other western legislatures to assure that United States senators were fully committed to the silver cause. The Nevadans tried to show their spirit in the latter proposal by reelecting William Morris Stewart in a unanimous vote.

Indeed, if the lawmakers seemed not to be observing the white metal's cause vigorously enough, they were soon reminded of their dereliction by the press. George Nixon asserted through the columns of the *Silver State* that *silver* was the "paramount issue"; the lawmakers must not petition Congress on any other topic—not the exciting proposals for a Nicaraguan canal, nothing that did not help the cause of their metal. Nixon underscored his argument: "If an advantage can be gained for silver by supporting the canal scheme, well and good, but if more can be gained by opposing it, we say oppose it." Nevertheless, the "canal scheme" did take a good deal of the legislators' attention, with memorials being framed, debated, amended, resubmitted, and argued again.[7] Regardless of these extra activities, however, the legislature of 1893 kept the pledge to reduce state expenditures.

The Silver party's first legislature attempted to cut expenses by consolidating some state offices and changing the responsibilities of others. These shifts saved the depression-ridden state an estimated $28,000 per year after they took effect. The lieutenant governor lost his $2,700 annual salary completely. The governor's salary was reduced from $5,000 to $4,000 per year. All deputy state officers' salaries were cut $800—from $2,000 to $1,200 per year. Similar savings were also effected in other departments.[8]

As the fifty-day session drew to a close, the Silverite press congratulated its partisans for a good performance. The meeting was free of scandal, wrote one editor, and pledges of financial retrenchment had been kept. "All in all," he concluded, "the Silver party has reason to be proud of its representatives."[9] Editor Nixon called the session hard-working and careful, pointing out that the members had met daily from 10:30 in the morning to 4:30 in the afternoon and had held two night meetings.[10] At Reno, the *Weekly Gazette and Stockman* editor opined that the legislature had accomplished nothing useful.[11]

Indeed, very little came of the first Silver session of the

legislature. The outburst of talk about promoting the white metal, and the memorial to Congress urging retention of the features of the Sherman Act that required purchase of silver bullion, were observed only in the breach. The irrigation act was repealed before anyone tried to make it effective. And, within the state, conditions continued to worsen.

Late in the summer, the mines of the Comstock struck "bare bones." The miners' union managed to hold the men's wages at four dollars per day and to keep the old ban against Chinese labor. But dividends on mining stocks were in the past, and salaries of the mine managers were halved.[12] The cuts in mine officers' wages were followed shortly by similar reductions in the salaries of employees on the Virginia and Truckee railroad.[13] By October, it was reported that the local passenger business on the V & T would be discontinued unless business improved.[14]

Meanwhile, Grover Cleveland, in office only a short time, determined to do his best to stop the depression at the national level. He called the Congress into special session and recommended repeal of the Sherman Silver Purchase Act of 1890, because, he said, he believed the depression "to be principally chargeable to congressional legislation touching the purchase and coinage of silver by the general government." The Sherman Act, said the president, did not allow the secretary of the Treasury to exercise the proper discretion and thus "the parity between gold and silver" was "disturbed." The problem of having to pay for silver bullion in gold, the president claimed, had caused a huge outflow of gold, a deficit in the balance of payments, a "falling off of confidence in the currency and the present depression." He urged Congress to make all possible haste in repealing the Sherman Act, requesting that there be no panic, but only "calm councils." Finally, he assured his auditors that the repealer would undo the "mischief" perpetrated by the Sherman Act.

Senator Stewart lost no time in arraigning the president. Stewart wrote, "The president's message is the most un-American document I ever read." Cleveland was abandoning the American people to the moneylenders and bondholders of Europe, the senator said. He felt that the solution to the depression was not to contract the currency by stopping the circulation of silver, but to expand the money supply. He promised to introduce a bill to that effect.[15]

At the same time, a number of easterners attacked Nevada's status as a state. Pointing out that the population had declined until it was less than that of a small eastern town, the antagonists suggested that statehood be withdrawn. Westerners answered the attacks on both constitutional and ethical grounds.[16] Neverthless, the eastern politicians and press continued to propose that Nevada be consolidated with Utah, Montana, and Idaho.[17]

Meanwhile, the westerners rallied to save their chief product. With the Sherman Act repealer in the House of Representatives on August 22, Francis G. Newlands spoke against the proposal. He told his listeners that since he was the sole representative of his party (Silver) in the House, he could not make a partisan appeal with any hope of commanding party loyalty. Therefore, he proposed to take a general view of the question. After surveying the international monetary situation, he addressed himself to industrial and financial conditions at the national level. Newlands declared that he could not understand the attitude of eastern railroad and banking interests in supporting the repeal. The railroads would certainly lose money if the West were impoverished by degradation of one of the section's chief products, for their greatest mileage lay over western lands. Then other interests would be affected, bringing "additional disaster to Eastern stock markets and capital." Concluding, Newlands claimed that silver should be the basis for expansion of the currency, or the United States would be further in debt internationally, would have an entire region poverty-stricken, and would ultimately suffer a deflation that would bring economic distress to the entire nation.[18] The repealer passed a few days later with the votes of administration Democrats and Republicans, despite the efforts of representatives from thirty states in the West and South.[19]

While the debate proceeded in Congress, New York's Cooper Union hall was the site of a silverite rally. About three thousand people assembled to hear an oration by one of the white metal's outstanding advocates, "Silver Dick" Bland. Bland could not attend, but a young congressman from Nebraska appeared as a substitute, making the principal address. The New York *Press* described the speech as "the best . . . made thus far in the extra session," and said prophetically, "Mr. Bryan is one of the coming men in Western politics."[20]

When the Sherman Act repealer arrived in the Senate, some silverites expressed hope for a compromise. Several senators said they would consider merely reducing the amount of silver to be purchased by the government, and thus not repeal the act completely. This discussion was effectively ended by word from the president; he absolutely refused to consider a change.

Meanwhile, thirty-three senators were ready to speak on

the proposal, William Stewart reserving one day, and John Percival Jones two days, for their addresses. Silverite senators planned a program that would prevent a vote unless their antagonists invoked cloture. Stewart then spoke for three full days. The *Silver State* editor claimed that the senator had "crowned himself with a wreath of immortal glory" in demonstrating that the enemies of silver were "bankrupt in morals, insolvent in principle, and paupers in patriotism."[21]

When Senator Jones spoke, it was to make his second great speech on silver. Jones, born in Wales, was a veteran of the Comstock's boom days, when he had been a mine superintendent. Product of the notoriously corrupt system by which some Nevada senators purchased their seats through the votes of a compliant legislature, Jones was seldom in the state and was never held in the affectionate regard that Stewart was at the time. The senior senator had no apparent interest except in the silver cause and an occasional poker game, no important committee assignments in the Senate, and no special partisan interests in Nevada.[22] A quiet, easygoing man who seldom spoke to newspapermen, he found it a simple matter to gain their attention, for when he did make a statement, the news seemed important. Jones spoke for seven days, and when it was printed, the dissertation was more than 450 pages long. He argued, in summary, that the quantity of money in circulation was the key to the country's relative prosperity; that gold, being in short supply, caused money to be too dear. Therefore, expansion of the currency would correct the problems of unemployment, underproduction, and depression.[23] Revolutionary in the 1890s, the ideas would sound like the commonplaces of economics a half century later.

The newspapers of the West followed the repeal controversy with great attention. Literally hundreds of articles appeared—all strongly partisan. Although the opposition to repeal of the Sherman Act continued in Congress for more than six weeks under the leadership of the senators from the West and South, it soon became obvious that the filibuster would collapse. Finally, on October 30, the gold-standard men in the Senate overcame the talkers and passed the repealer 43 votes to 32. The House concurred in amendments, and the president signed the bill.[24]

Cleveland's forcing of the Sherman Act repeal not only split the Democratic party, but also started the sectionalism on the silver issue that became more obvious later. The West and South had become firm allies against the president, while the East and North supported him. After the repeal, President Cleveland expected the panic to subside and the depression to end. When it did not, he was puzzled, but remained adamant for hard money.[25]

William Stewart presently severed his connections with the Republican party, and announced that he would thenceforth support the Populists nationally. In making his statement, Stewart expressed his version of the philosophy of the People's party: "The issue is momentous. The success of money power means falling prices, poverty and misery for the masses. . . . It is the duty of every patriot . . . to resist the cruel aggression and warfare which capital is now making against labor and the producers of wealth."[26]

When John Percival Jones followed Stewart the next year, the GOP in Nevada demanded that he resign his post in the Senate. Jones had chosen the correct side, however, for the

Silvermen called him "brave," "statesmanlike," and "without a peer, with the exception of Senator Stewart."[27]

All of these events could only strengthen the Silver party in Nevada. An interviewer from the *Appeal* accosted C. C. Wallace and inquired about the status of the party in the eastern section of the state. Wallace replied: "Well, from Eureka to the sink of the Humboldt you can't find a soul that don't look forward to another chance to go to the polls a year from this fall and smite the Philistines again. The few men who followed their party last fall are now with us solid. We are simply a homogenous mass of silver people. . . .[*sic*]" The lobbyist promised a full Silver slate for the next year's election.[28]

The Silvermen inaugurated the year's political season late in May, 1894, at a meeting of the party central committee. The group issued an address to the people of the state, recalling the history of the silver movement and indicating election plans. Because of the "base servility of the old parties . . . to the gold trust" the Silvermen desired unity of all supporters of the white metal. It was necessary, they said, to continue the independent party organization until they could hope for relief from the economic distress caused by the "silver crime." The party chiefs named September 4 as the date for the biennial convention, to be held in Carson City.

The national economic trouble was dramatized during the early spring when elements of "General" Jacob Coxey's "Industrial Army" passed through Nevada on the way to Washington, D.C. This demonstration had as its purpose to call the nation's attention to the plight of able-bodied persons who were starving or in poverty when the country had abundant natural resources. The group, estimated at a thousand when it left California, and at thirteen hundred after recruiting in Nevada, crossed the state in a special train of twenty-three cattle cars.[29]

A second indication of economic problems in the nation occurred in the summer, when workers struck the Pullman Company and a number of other railroad installations. As the strike spread across the country, many communities grew increasingly tense. After the disturbances had continued for a week, the editor at the railroad town of Winnemucca was certain that the nation was "on the verge of a revolution."[30] Troops were called into action in several cities. The situation in California was particularly critical, with the union leaders issuing manifestos and the government threatening to impose martial law. When the strike evolved into rioting and bloodletting, the Winnemucca editor predicted that the revolution would surely come, saying that "Senator Stewart has long contended that the revolution would be the end of long years of oppression under which the people have worn the yoke of the money power."[31] A week later, the same editor wrote that George M. Pullman, president of the railway car company, would "some day have to answer before the bar of judgment." His great wealth had "made him arrogant and he no doubt believe[d] himself omnipotent."[32]

The editor of the *Silver State* needed only to look around him to see local evidence of the strike. Several Nevada railroad towns were virtually under martial law. Winnemucca, for example, was host to some 250 regular army men who took over the railroad's property there. This, despite the fact that demonstrations in the city had been peaceful.[33] Further west at Wadsworth, however, some difficulties erupted. In the wake of damage to a number of locomotives, a troop of soldiers charged into a crowd with fixed bayonets. At the same time in Reno, excitement became concern when the troops served as targets for bad eggs thrown by local demonstrators.[34]

The presence of federal forces caused a great deal of resentment in Nevada. A group of citizens petitioned Governor Colcord to use his office to have the soldiers removed. The governor refused, saying that President Cleveland had acted legally in ordering the troops. A protest, therefore, he wrote, "would not only be of no use, but would, in my judgment, be unwise." Colcord cautioned the people not to resist or obstruct the soldiers, "otherwise the sympathies of our people for the oppressed in this unfortunate affair will be of no avail."[35]

The Silverite press castigated the governor for this refusal to demand the withdrwal of the army. Nixon wrote, "Let the change from puppets to men be peacefully inaugurated in November. Nevada needs a governor."[36] As for the government's expense in the operation, editor Nixon called it an "expenditure of public force for private benefit." He suggested that public ownership of the railroads would prevent such domestic violence as had occurred.[37] Thus the Silver party had several issues upon which to base its first campaign for state offices.

All over the nation in 1894, state political conventions displayed the force of the silver issue. From Maine and Vermont, Pennsylvania and Ohio, Kansas and Indiana, and finally from California came Republican party resolutions endorsing free coinage of silver.[38] Meanwhile, the Democrats did the same in their meetings, although occasional divisions occurred. In Nebraska, the Democrats split between silverites and administration men. A few state Democratic parties endorsed President Cleveland.[39] There was thus no substantial difference between the two major parties within the states; the silver question made interior divisions, but did not become a partisan issue until later.

In Nevada, however, where now the population was probably not over 45,000, and the effective electorate less than 11,000,[40] there were three major parties. The Republicans held their state convention first. As they met, it was obvious that the GOP was severely depleted. Only seven delegates arrived from the eastern and central parts of the state, while Eureka, Lander, and Nye counties sent no delegates at all. The convention lasted only a single evening, with all business disposed of quickly. Nevertheless, if the enthusiasm was a little forced, the Republicans managed to present the voters with a full slate of candidates for office, nominating former congressman Bartine for a chance to retake the seat from Francis G. Newlands, A. C. Cleveland for governor, and a full panel for other posts. The candidates were all loyal party men, and at another time the slate would have had a good chance to sweep the state. The platform called for free coinage of silver at 16 to 1, endorsed the idea of arbitration in labor disputes, and charged the Silver party with various political crimes and errors, including subservience to the railroad.[41]

When they met in September, 1894, the Democrats were as faction-ridden as they had been two years before. The first convention was called by a splinter group under the leadership of Robert Keating of Storey County and Hirsch Harris, an employee of the mint at Carson City. The majority of the delegates at this so-called Mugwump convention were employed either by Keating or by the mint. They nominated Keating for governor, J. E. Gignoux for Congress, and several others.[42]

The regular, or "genuine," Democrats also met in Carson City, under the leadership of John H. Dennis, chairman of the state central committee. The delegations at this regular Democratic assembly were not large, although more persons attended than had appeared at the "splinter" convention. Dennis made the opening speech at the meeting, excoriating the Democrats who had deserted the party for Silver. He claimed that these men had betrayed their own party in joining the Silvermen, and were, in 1894, trying to return to the old ranks to receive political favors. Expected to be certified as the regular Democratic nominees (despite the splinter Mugwumps) were enough candidates to fill the slate. The platform called for free coinage of silver at sixteen to one, and favored arbitration of labor disputes. Then the disunited Democrats endorsed the administration of the archenemy of silver, Grover Cleveland.[43]

Well might the Democracy have been demoralized. The week before they met, the Silver party chiefs had assembled. At "the most enthusiastic gathering ever held in Carson," the Silvermen adopted a platform and nominated a full slate of candidates for state offices. The platform made the usual declarations in favor of remonetization of silver, and put the party on record in favor of government ownership of railroads (i.e., foreclosure on the roads' bonds), compulsory arbitration of labor disputes, and direct election of senators. The Silvermen commended Stewart, Jones, and Newlands for services to the party and to the state.[44]

The Silver convention delegates were enthusiastic about their cause and certain of winning the forthcoming election, but the gathering was not completely harmonious. A

Washoe County representative introduced a proposal to have the Silver party become affiliated with the national People's party, with appropriate change in name. The motion was tabled. Then Francis Newlands, newly nominated for Congress, gave a speech in which he did not fully support the platform. He endorsed the silver cause, but opposed government ownership of railroads on the ground that it had been unsatisfactory where tried. The speech somewhat diminished the spirit of the delegates, including Thomas Wren, who refused to applaud.[45] The speech also offended C. C. Wallace, who virtually ordered Newlands to abandon this line and to adhere to the platform. A pro-railroad stand by the party leaders, Wallace told the candidate, would interfere with the railroad's plans.[46] The railroad thus demonstrated that its chiefs had no objection to anti-railroad declarations from the party they controlled. Elections were to be won, and postelection actions need not adhere to preelection talk. Newlands obliged his critics on both sides by promising to support the platform or resign.[47] Still another problem arose when James Doughty, a railroad man from Elko, and B. F. Curler, an attorney from Reno, tried to secure nominations from the Silver party. They reportedly threatened to organize a People's party in the state if their requests were denied. They failed at the Silver convention and withdrew.[48]

Along with Newlands, the nominees of the Silvermen included John Edward Jones for governor and Reinhold Sadler for lieutenant governor. In the full slate, nominees from the eastern counties dominated the ticket's major places.[49] Seven former Democrats[50] and five former Republicans[51] gained the top places.

Two other parties convened before the fall elections.

The People's party, supposedly rejected by the silverites, organized a small but enthusiastic group who nominated nearly a complete slate of candidates. Selected to run for office under the Populist banner were James Doughty for Congress, "Farmer" George Peckham of Washoe County for governor, B. F. Curler for district judge, and others from rural communities in Douglas and Lincoln counties.[52] The Populists said they were true to the silver cause and claimed that they never wished to split the silverite vote; their stated purpose in organizing was said to be to make it possible to present presidential electors pledged to the national party in the election two years hence.[53] They also deplored what they considered the obvious influence of the railroad in Silver party councils.[54] The Prohibition party of Nevada failed to qualify any candidates for the general election ballot, but adopted a platform that, in addition to condemning strong spirits, endorsed free coinage of silver at 16 to 1.[55]

The ensuing campaign, while spirited, was generally one-sided. The Silvermen, having raided both major parties, had nearly all of the best and most experienced politicians in the state. The gubernatorial candidate, John Edward Jones, for example, had been in state politics for nearly a decade as surveyor general. The second man on the Silver ticket was almost equally well known.

Reinhold Sadler, like Jones, was an immigrant to the United States. Born in Czarnikow, Prussia, in 1848, Sadler had come to Nevada to work for an uncle who operated a chain of mercantile stores in the state and in California. As a young man, Sadler became very astute in business management and ultimately quite wealthy. He joined the Democrats when he was old enough to vote and stayed with the party through the next two decades. Sadler was a candidate, usually unsuccessful, for Eureka County or state office at every election after he became a resident until 1892, when the Silver party began to monopolize his attention. He was regarded as an effective and sincere speaker, although his German accent was often the butt of local jokes.[56]

Jones's Republican opponent, Abner C. Cleveland, had been in the state since 1863. A native of Maine, he emigrated to California in the 1850s. There, he worked as a miner and stock raiser. In Nevada, he mined on the Comstock and owned a lumber operation in Washoe County. Cleveland was a county commissioner of Washoe County in 1866 and was elected a member of the legislature from the same county in 1868. Later that same year, he moved to White Pine County in eastern Nevada, where he established a profitable ranching and stock-raising operation, engaged in an occasional promotion to bring in a railroad, and served as the county's state senator.[57] Cleveland was probably the only nominee of any party in opposition to the Silvermen who had even a remote chance of election in 1894.

The Republicans began their canvass on September 22 with a rally in Reno. A bonfire lighted the street, a cannon boomed, and Horace F. Bartine and A. C. Cleveland made major speeches. The candidates pledged their best efforts to the cause of free silver and endorsed the Republican state platform.[58]

The Silver party's adherents met at the same place a few days later for the initiation of their campaign. At that time many Populists were astounded to find that a number of their trusted leaders had deserted to the Silverites, even taking prominent parts in the conduct of the rally. Clearly, a division had occurred among the Populists, a split traceable to a Republican effort to defeat the Silvermen by political maneuver. The results of the plot were illustrated in the campaign. Judge William Webster, who had presided at the People's party state convention, was now the presiding officer for the Silvermen. Webster made the first speech, saying that while James Doughty, the Populist candidate for Congress, was a fine young man, it was the duty of the voters of Nevada to support Francis Newlands. He also endorsed John E. Jones for governor, neglecting even to mention "Farmer" Peckham's candidacy. Newlands and Thomas Wren made the other orations at the rally.[59] The Silver party of Nevada then began its appeal to the voters. The Democrats took only a minor part in the campaign, for their ranks had been decimated by defections to the Silvermen.

The congressional canvass was particularly interesting, featuring what amounted to a three-cornered race among Bartine, Newlands, and Doughty. B. F. Riley, the Democrat, had no honest hope of election. The Republicans had reportedly manipulated their organization and the People's party to ensure the defeat of Newlands. Doughty, the Populist, had several attributes that seemed to promise a fairly good tally. He was a railroad striker in the summer of 1894, and now posed as a poor man waging a heavy fight against the wealthy Francis Newlands. The people in the state's railroad towns were sympathetic with the strike and were expected to vote for Doughty, drawing votes from Newlands. Bartine was a pioneer politician, then out of office as congressman. Even though defeated by Stewart for the Senate two years before, he confidently expected to win

the congressional post in 1894. Then some leaders of the
national People's party discovered the Republican plot
and tried to convince the Nevada Populists to withdraw
Doughty's nomination in the interest of silverite unity.
Doughty refused, however, and continued to campaign
despite the fact that nearly everyone felt that he would lose
the election.[60] The sincere supporters of free coinage deserted then to the Silver party.

Meanwhile, the "gold bug" press supported the Populists
only slightly less enthusiastically than it did the Republicans.
The GOP leaders hoped thus to divide the silverite vote
enough to gain the election for themselves. The Republican
state chairman, Trenmor Coffin, wrote and received several
communications confirming the plan. C. H. Sproule, editor
of the *Elko Free Press,* said in one message: "I think our
best fight here will be to draw all the votes we can for the
Populists. They are bound to come from the Silver ranks,
and I don't think a single vote will be drawn from the
Republican side. . . ."[61] A party worker in Storey County
assured Coffin that "the Silver-Pops [*sic*] and the Democrats" would divide only the vote left over after the Republican victory.[62]

Only a few members of the GOP failed to support the
plan. Alex Wise, a successful candidate for the state senate
from Humboldt County, wrote that because of the strength
of Silver sentiment in his county, he would run as an independent and support the Republicans privately.[63] The owner
of a Populist newspaper in Pioche, a candidate for state
printer on the People's party ticket, wrote to Coffin that
he was doing his best for the cause in southern Nevada,
charging the opponents more for advertising than he charged
the Republicans.[64] A Silverite editor wrote that the rail-

road's representatives had conceived the scheme of dividing the white metal's supporters. By this interpretation, the corporation's best interests were served by the GOP.[65] The Silverite press thus maintained the antirailroad posture that the Central Pacific was said to desire.

Few of the Republicans wore the railroad label openly. A. C. Cleveland, campaigning in the central part of the state, told his audiences that he had tried to build a railroad to compete with the Central Pacific in Nevada. He had raised $50,000 from financiers in California and had engaged surveyors. Because of the depression, however, the project was abandoned.[66] Despite this attempt, or perhaps because he had redeemed himself later in a lobbying partnership with Black Wallace, the corporation, or "money powers," did not oppose Cleveland; he was expected to be elected with their help.[67]

The Republican attempt to reestablish control and break the Silvermen failed with the Silver party's effective and ultimately successful campaign in 1894. In spite of a generous outlay of money and an attempt late in the canvass to inject accusations of corruption against Jones, the gubernatorial candidate, the GOP lost every race by substantial margins.[68] The Democrats polled fewer than 825 votes in their best race, and the only Populist who received a convincing tally was Doughty, who nevertheless ran third after Newlands and Bartine.[69] The Silver party, better managed and better financed, took every place for which it offered a candidate, at a reported cost of slightly more than $1.33 per voter for the party, or $7,684.62, most of which Francis G. Newlands paid.[70]

The election brought a new person to every state office. Only the governor-elect, John Edward Jones, had served in a state post; all other newly-elected officials were amateurs or had been in county or town offices. Similarly, the legislature had few experienced men; only two assemblymen and six senators (who had longer terms) had served before.[71] At the end of the campaign, the Silver party men celebrated their victory at a grand governor's "inaugural ball." Decorations for the occasion offered the motif of the party symbolized by a stack of silver bricks. These were discovered, rather appropriately in view of continuing railroad influence, to be silver-painted railroad ties.[72]

The anticlimax to the election victory was soon to come. The Silvermen who controlled the state government had based their campaign on a demand for several reforms and would presumably now convert promises to action. The performance, however, would fall somewhat short of expectations, setting a pattern for other sessions that would follow during the next several years.

As the time approached for the seventeenth session of the Nevada legislature to convene, the editor of one of the leading Silver newspapers wrote a thoughtful article, indicating his ideas of what the session might accomplish. Remarking on the depression still current in the region, the *Nevada State Journal* writer proposed that the state constitution might be amended to reflect the deteriorating conditions. He suggested, too, that expenses could be reduced by requiring state printing to be done within the state, rather than at San Francisco. A reduction in the number of state employees in such positions as deputies and attachés was another recommendation. Finally, he urged the legislature to conduct its business speedily, in less than the allotted sixty days.[73]

When the session opened, the houses received messages

from several members of the state government. Governor Colcord, retiring from office, decried the "total abandonment of silver as money," which he said had caused the depression to worsen. He predicted, however, that relief would come, and with it "free coinage of silver, cheaper transportation, the opening up of other mining and agricultural districts by the building of new railroads and the establishment of manufactories in our midst. . . ." Then, he said, the people of Nevada would "be in a position to reap the reward which we have so justly earned by our patience. . . ."[74]

Governor Jones's inaugural address, delivered to the opening session of the legislature, reflected his Populist philosophy. He deplored the "silver crime" but said that the real cause for the depression was that the "corporate money powers" had "almost absorbed the prosperity of the country." The workers of the nation, he asserted, were in danger of enslavement by the owners of the means of production. Jones praised attempts to organize the workers, saying that labor was "actuated by the purest motives, and the highest behests of judgment and conscience." After again condemning the "money powers still controlling our National administration," the new governor touched upon proposals for promotion of home industries and recommended expansion of educational opportunities.[75]

The party leaders of both houses also spoke briefly. The new lieutenant governor, Reinhold Sadler, presiding over the senate by constitutional prerogative, urged action leading to remonetization of silver. Lem Allen of Churchill County, the speaker of the assembly, asked only that the late political strife be forgotten in a united effort to revive the state's economy.[76] The first Silver legislature was ready for business.

The session outwardly appeared to be largely routine, with the members adhering to a number of charges made by the governor. The houses approved a bill allowing the establishment of county high schools in the state and authorized the building of dormitories at the state university, thereby giving the requested expansion of educational opportunities. The legislators acted upon a proposal to cause the label of the International Typographical Union to be placed on all state printing, thus showing their sympathy with organized labor. Probably the outstanding action of the session was the enactment of a "purity of elections" law, requiring disclosure of moneys expended in political campaigns and outlining what would henceforth be considered corrupt activities in state politics.[77] The Silverites accordingly recorded their firm opposition to the disgraceful practices then current in the West. The real action of the session was neither routine nor colorless, however, and involved some truly interesting performances.

Early in the session, Governor Jones received a telegram from the *Chicago Tribune* asking, "What is the most important measure now before your Legislature and the chances for it passing." Jones replied, "Resolution against the Reilly Funding bill. Result doubtful."[78] The background of this controversy had affected state and national politics for some years. In 1893, the Nevada legislature passed, over Governor Colcord's veto, a resolution favoring the refunding of the debts of the Pacific Coast railroads. That is, the legislators then favored the issuance of government bonds to pay the roads' creditors. Observers then and later concluded that this action proved that the railroad controlled Nevada

politics. The same legislature elected William M. Stewart
to a new term in the United States Senate. At the time, said
one writer, the senator "plumed himself upon the fact" that
he was a paid employee of the Southern Pacific. Concurrently, C. C. Wallace was Stewart's campaign manager and
the railroad's salaried lobbyist.[79] In 1895, the Reilly bill in
Congress provided another opportunity for Nevada politicians to record their sentiments toward the railroad.

The Reilly Funding Bill provided for the securing of
fifty-year, 2 percent bonds on the debts of the government-
subsidized Pacific Coast railroads. The Silvermen publicly
opposed the Reilly bill, favoring instead—in accordance
with their platform—the foreclosure of government liens on
the roads and ultimately their ownership or management
by the government.[80] Reminding the Silver party legislators
of their published pledge, the leading Silver newspaper
editor in Reno demanded that the legislature memorialize
the Congress to defeat the Reilly bill.[81]

On the third day of the session, Senator H. A. Comins
of White Pine County introduced Senate Concurrent Resolution 3, demanding that the Nevada congressional delegation seek the collection of the Pacific Coast railroads' debts.
The resolution further urged that the Interstate Commerce
Commission regulations be enforced everywhere "so that
unjust discrimination may be prohibited. . . ."[82] The latter
provision reflected conditions in the state, where ICC regulations forbidding larger fees for short hauls than for long
ones were suspended.[83] The resolution passed the senate on
the same day it was introduced. Through parliamentary
maneuvering, the resolution was considered again and
passed a second time. The senate concurred in amendments
from the assembly and again passed the resolution. Two

weeks after the introduction of SCR 3, the governor reported having signed it.[84]

Throughout the debate and maneuvering in both houses, a great deal of excitement was evident in all sections of the state. Crowds of people sat in the galleries of the chambers, listening to the speeches and watching the action. The railroad's advocates were always present, pressing the case for the corporation on all resolutions and legislation.[85] The ultimate disposition of the Reilly bill resolution was relatively unimportant at that time; therefore the railroad could afford to lose—and did lose—the skirmish. The battle on the funding bill thus ended with the Silvermen ostensibly fulfilling their pledges in the impotent memorial to Congress. Congressman Newlands took the legislature's petition seriously and voted continually against funding proposals in the House.[86] In the state legislature, railroad representatives continued to be active. At the end of the session, moreover, Thomas Wren wrote that the corporation's lobbyists had taken advantage of some individuals who were "corrupt and weak and inexperienced" to secure the company's objectives on local legislation.[87]

A second center of interest during the legislature's seventeenth session, at least to a large minority of the state's residents, was the possibility that women might be granted the privilege of voting. Mrs. Frances Williamson was a prime leader of the suffrage forces in Nevada. An 1863 pioneer of Austin, Mrs. Williamson was one of the camp's first public school teachers. Her marriage to J. R. Williamson began an association that led both to politics: Williamson as state senator from Lander County, and his wife as the leader of women in the state in their drive for enfranchisement. In the early excitement over the creation of silver clubs, Mrs. Williamson formed a Women's Silver League in Austin and attempted with some success to make the group a statewide organization.[88]

When the legislative session was about three weeks old, the women demonstrated support for a proposed constitutional amendment to remove the word "male" from voting requirements. They arranged for a national leader in the suffrage movement, Mila Tupper Maynard, to speak to the Nevada lawmakers on the topic of women's rights. The gallery filled with supporters, including the wives of three past and present governors of the state, Mrs. John E. Jones, Mrs. R. K. Colcord, and Mrs. Jewett Adams, and the wives of various legislators.

The women won a point in 1895. The legislators approved a resolution for amending the constitution. The next legal requirement was passage by the following session of the legislature, and then a favorable ballot by the voters of the state.[89] This encouragement led the women to convene that autumn in Reno to organize the State League of Woman Suffrage and elect Mrs. Williamson as president.[90]

The legislature meanwhile adjourned. Except for the purity of elections law, the woman suffrage resolution, and the harmless but politically acute resolution on the Reilly bill, little was accomplished. Sam Davis of the *Morning Appeal* blamed the scarcity of effective legislation on opponents of the Silvermen, who obstructed all attempts at reform in an effort to embarrass the party in power.[91] Thomas Wren blamed the railroad.

Governor Jones, at the head of the state administration, made several attempts at least to improve the state's economy. The year 1895 was the worst in the depression to that time. In 1894, mining output had struck an all-time low, and this was followed by drastic decreases in livestock and grain prices.[92] At the same time, the state's population continued to decline, as did the assessed valuation of properties.[93] Jones, an advocate of reclamation of desert and waste lands in the arid region, believed that with proper instruction new settlers could be brought into the state. He wrote that many people had expressed interest in Nevada lands, and that a number of relatively unknown areas could be irrigated and cultivated if settlers were told about correct methods.[94] He also replied to many requests for information about farm plots in the state, usually in the same spirit. Jones continued as well to express his devotion to the silver cause, writing letters and holding meetings in a search for ideas in support of the white metal.[95]

The governor would never know how his plans might have profited the people of Nevada. Before the end of his first year in office, his health failed. In November, 1895, he left the state, hoping to be cured in California, and Lieutenant Governor Reinhold Sadler assumed the office. He soon became governor of Nevada in duty, and ultimately made the title his own.

NOTES

[1] *Silver State,* November 29, 1892, p. 2.

[2] See Appendix I.

[3] Nevada, Surveyor General, "Biennial Report of the Surveyor General and State Land Register, 1891–1892," State Printing Office, 1893.

[4] *Nevada State Journal,* January 5, 1893, p. 3.

[5] Nevada, State Legislature, *Appendix to the Journals of the Senate and Assembly,* Sixteenth Session (1893). Governor Colcord's message.

[6] *Silver State,* January 17, 1893, p. 2.

[7] *Ibid.,* February 1 to February 18, 1893, *passim.*
[8] *Nevada State Journal,* January 27, 1897, p. 2.
[9] *Silver State,* March 7, 1893, p. 2.
[10] *Ibid.,* February 14, 1893, p. 3.
[11] *Reno Weekly Gazette and Stockman,* March 16, 1893, p. 4.
[12] *Silver State,* July 22, 1893, p. 3.
[13] *Ibid.,* August 14, 1893, p. 3.
[14] *Ibid.,* October 23, 1893, p. 3.
[15] *Ibid.,* August 10, 1893, pp. 2 and 3.
[16] *Ibid.,* August 11, 1893, p. 2.
[17] *Ibid.,* September 27, 1893, p. 2.
[18] *Ibid.,* September 6, 1893, pp. 2–3.
[19] *Ibid.,* August 28 and August 29, 1893, *passim.*
[20] *Ibid.,* August 30, 1893, p. 3 (reprinted).
[21] *Ibid.,* September 9 through 18, 1893, *passim.*
[22] Gilman Ostrander, *Nevada, The Great Rotten Borough, 1859–1964* (New York: Alfred A. Knopf, 1966), pp. 69–70, 104–105; *Silver State,* May 21, 1892, p. 3.
[23] John Percival Jones, "The Remonetization of Silver," Speech by the Hon. John P. Jones in the Senate of the United States, October 14, 16, 21, 23, 24, 27, and 30, 1893 (463 pp.).
[24] *Silver State,* September–October, 1893, *passim.*
[25] J. Rogers Hollingsworth, *The Whirligig of Politics* (Chicago: University of Chicago Press, 1963), pp. 16–18. For a sympathetic account of Cleveland's problems in connection with the Sherman Act repeal, see Rexford G. Tugwell, *Grover Cleveland* (New York: Macmillan Company, 1968), pp. 202–212.
[26] *Silver State,* September 21, 1893, p. 3.
[27] *Ibid.,* September 7 and 18, 1894, *passim.*
[28] *Ibid.,* September 7, 1893, p. 3.
[29] *Ibid.,* April 9, 1894, p. 3.
[30] *Ibid.,* July 3, 1894, p. 2.
[31] *Ibid.,* July 7, 1894, p. 2.
[32] *Ibid.,* July 13, 1894, p. 2.
[33] *Ibid.,* July 14, 1894, pp. 2 and 3.
[34] *Reno Evening Gazette,* July 16, 1894, p. 3.
[35] *Silver State,* July 17, 1894, p. 3.
[36] *Ibid.,* July 20, 1894, p. 2.
[37] *Ibid.,* July 21, 1894, p. 2.
[38] Lawrence John Scheidler, "Silver and Politics, 1893–1896" (Ph.D. dissertation, Indiana University, 1936).

[39] *Ibid.,* pp. 108–113.

[40] See Appendix II.

[41] *Reno Evening Gazette,* August 25, 1894, p. 1.

[42] *Ibid.,* September 12 and September 13, 1894, *passim.*

[43] *Ibid.,* September 15, 1894, p. 3.

[44] *Morning Appeal,* September 5, 1894, p. 2.

[45] *Reno Evening Gazette,* September 5, 1894, p. 1.

[46] Francis G. Newlands to William F. Herrin [1900]. Newlands papers.

[47] *Reno Evening Gazette,* September 5, 1894, p. 1.

[48] *Silver State,* October 17, 1894, pp. 2 and 3.

[49] *Reno Evening Gazette,* September 5, 1894, pp. 1 and 2.

[50] *Ibid.,* September 7, 1894, p. 3.

[51] *Nevada State Journal,* January 8, 1895, p. 2.

[52] *Reno Evening Gazette,* September 7, 1894, p. 1.

[53] *Ibid.,* October 3, 1894, p. 3.

[54] *Silver State,* October 17, 1894, pp. 2 and 3; *Reno Evening Gazette,* August 22, 1894, p. 3.

[55] *Reno Evening Gazette,* October 9, 1894, p. 3.

[56] Myrtle Myles, "Fortune for a Governor," *Las Vegas Review-Journal, The Nevadan* (supplement), May 24, 1964, p. 4; *White Pine News,* September 27, 1890, p. 3; *Eureka Sentinel,* July 24, 1878, p. 3.

[57] M. Angel, ed., *History of Nevada,* p. 188; Nevada, Secretary of State, *Political History of Nevada, 1965,* p. 146.

[58] *Reno Evening Gazette,* September 24, 1894, p. 3.

[59] *Ibid.,* October 2, 1894, p. 3.

[60] Samuel P. Davis, "Political Revolution in Nevada," *San Francisco Call,* November 3, 1895, p. 17.

[61] C. H. Sproule to Trenmor Coffin, September 14, 1894. Coffin papers.

[62] W. T. Cuddy to Trenmor Coffin, October 22, 1894. Coffin papers.

[63] Alex Wise to W. R. Randall, secretary of the Republican state central committee, October 17, 1894. Coffin papers.

[64] N. P. Dooley to Trenmor Coffin, October 31, 1894. Coffin papers.

[65] *Silver State,* September 12, 1894, p. 2.

[66] *Ibid.,* October 1, 1894, p. 2.

[67] Trenmor Coffin to the *New York World* (telegram) [October, 1894]. Coffin papers.

[68] *Carson Morning News* (Carson City, Nevada), September 13, 1894, p. 3; September 16, 1894, p. 2; *Morning Appeal,* September 14, 1894, p. 2; September 16, 1894, p. 2.

[69] Nevada, Secretary of State, *Political History of Nevada, 1965,* p. 184.

[70] "Balance sheet of the Silver Party, 1894," ms. Newlands papers.

[71] Nevada, Secretary of State, *Political History of Nevada, 1965,* p. 135.

[72] *Territorial Enterprise,* February 27, 1895, p. 3.

[73] *Nevada State Journal,* January 20, 1895, p. 2.

[74] Nevada, State Legislature, *Appendix to the Journals of the Senate and Assembly,* Seventeenth Session (1895). Governor Colcord's message.

[75] *Ibid.,* Governor Jones's message.

[76] *Nevada State Journal,* January 22, 1895, p. 3.

[77] Nevada, State Legislature, *Statutes of Nevada, 1895.*

[78] Letter box, "Letters to the Governor's office, 1893–1898." Nevada Historical Society, Reno, Nevada.

[79] *Reno Evening Gazette,* August 22, 1894, p. 2.

[80] *Nevada State Journal,* January 18, 1895, p. 2.

[81] *Ibid.,* January 24, 1895, p. 2.

[82] Nevada, State Legislature, *Statutes of Nevada, 1895.*

[83] *Nevada State Journal,* January 18, 1895, p. 2.

[84] Nevada State Legislature, *Journal of the State,* Seventeenth Session, 1895. Two years after the discussion over the Reilly bill, Sardis Summerfield, legislative leader of the railroad forces, had strong support from Senator Stewart and C. C. Wallace for the appointment as U.S. district attorney for Nevada. See Stewart papers, 1897.

[85] *Nevada State Journal,* January 24, 1895, to February 1, 1895, *passim.*

[86] Francis G. Newlands to William F. Herrin [1900]. Newlands papers.

[87] *Nevada State Journal,* March 22, 1895, p. 3.

[88] *Silver State,* August 16, 1893, p. 3; *Morning Appeal,* January 12, 1899, p. 3.

[89] *Nevada State Journal,* February 12, 1895, p. 3; March 19, 1895, p. 2.

[90] *Reno Evening Gazette,* October 29 to October 31, 1895, *passim.*

[91] *Nevada State Journal,* February 18, 1895, p. 3 (reprinted).

[92] See Appendix I.

[93] James G. Scrugham, ed., *Nevada,* 3 vols. (Chicago: American Historical Society, 1935) I, 367.

[94] John Edward Jones to Clayton Belknap, June 14, 1895. In letter box, "Letters to the Governor's office, 1893–1898." Nevada Historical Society, Reno.

[95] See letters and telegrams in "Governor's Office Letter Book (Jones, Sadler, Allen, Sparks)," Nevada Historical Society, Reno. See especially: John E. Jones to James H. Budd, April 18, 1895; Jones to the *Chicago Tribune,* July 5, 1895.

V

The Election of 1896 and
Its Aftermath

THE OFF-YEAR balloting in 1895 in the nation offered little encouragement to the silverites. Republicans took leading positions after local elections in several eastern and middle western states. In Nevada, the Republican victories were hailed as a repudiation of President Grover Cleveland's "sound money" attitudes, and a rebuke to the national Democratic party's equivocations on free coinage.[1] Nevertheless, the advancement of Republican "gold bugs" was hardly a favorable portent for advocates of remonetization.

Another sign, unfavorable to silver, came when the United States Senate organized for its new session and Populists voted with Republicans. The Populists held positions of power in the Senate, where the committee appointments were divided among forty-two Republicans, eleven Democrats, and six Populists or Silvermen.[2]

Concurrently, support for the white metal came from other sources. Henry M. Teller, still favoring free coinage in spite of his earlier defection to the gold-standard man, Benjamin Harrison, reported receiving petitions bearing thousands of signatures from various branches of the American Federation of Labor. Inevitably, the documents asked "justice" for silver.[3] In April, 1896, Francis G. Newlands spoke to a meeting of the House Committee on Ways and Means in a presentation of the case for the white metal. In the talk, the Nevada congressman showed that the low price of silver in the United States had caused an unfavorable balance of trade. Forcing down prices of farm products by depressing the price of the metal caused, in turn, lower returns for American goods abroad. Free coinage, Newlands argued, would raise prices of both silver and exports, and the adverse balance and depressed farm economy would thereby be relieved. The committee members were interested in Newlands's reasoning, and thought his ideas novel enough to hold their attention for more than two hours, but not to gain their support.[4]

Little real hope existed for free silver unless its advocates could capture the national administration. Senator William Stewart received a letter from an editor in Ohio explaining: "Because our paper [the *Chagrin Falls Exponent*] advocates free coinage we find it difficult to procure public documents. Could I trouble you have sent to me copy of last report of the Director of the mint . . . [and the] last Statistical Abstracts. . . ." The writer concluded optimistically, however, that "free silver sentiment is spreading and intensifying here in Sherman's old stronghold."[5]

The Nevada congressional delegation had several problems caused by the position its members had taken on the financial question. William Stewart wrote in March, 1896, that the two senators and Congressman Newlands had great difficulty in performing even routine patronage chores for their constituents because of their stand on free silver.[6] Realizing that the answer to these troubles lay in promoting action at the national level, Stewart and Newlands involved themselves in the work of the National Silver party. This organization was proposed as a new political party to supplant the nearly defunct and determinedly nonpartisan Bimetallic Union and similar organizations.[7]

The plan advanced by the silver men was for all supporters of free coinage to merge their organizations into a national party. The group decided to form committees in all major cities to work for the fusion of local forces, raise money, and distribute propaganda. The new party planned to meet in St. Louis on July 22, 1896, the opening day of the People's party convention in the same city. All delegates were democratically elected—not appointed by some organization.[8]

Senator Stewart was quite optimistic about the prospects for the success of this plan. He apparently thought that silver supporters were a majority of voters in the nation, and that they would bestow their confidence on the new party. In February, he wrote to a friend in Utah, "This is the first time that I have really seen light ahead. . . ."[9] The next month, he wrote to C. C. Wallace, "I say the prospects are good to win [the presidency] . . . but if we do not win [that], we will win enough to settle the question that financial reformers will soon get possession of the Government."[10]

The Republican party held its national convention in June, 1896, in St. Louis. The gathering offered a final opportunity for the GOP to take over the free-silver movement. In spite of serious and determined efforts by westerners, however, it became obvious that the Republicans would declare for "sound money." A St. Louis reporter asked a member of the Nevada delegation what might happen in the event of the adoption of a platform that contained a gold-standard plank. The delegate replied, "We are all for silver, of course, as everyone in Nevada is. We intend to make a fight for silver [on the floor of the convention]. But if this convention should declare for the single gold standard I suppose we would have to stand it. There is nothing else we could do."[11] That was a weak statement in view of what happened within only a few hours.

When the platform of the Republican party was presented to the delegates, it contained the "sound money" plank that westerners had feared. Senator Henry M. Teller offered a "silver amendment" which was defeated in committee by a vote of forty-one to ten. Senator Frank J. Cannon of Utah grimly faced the convention and read a long statement declaring that in adopting a gold-standard plank, the Republicans were violating their traditions. The booing and hissing that greeted his proclamation made it virtually impossible for the chairman to restore order. The silver men then left the convention. Henry Teller, Fred T. Dubois of Idaho, and Cannon led their entire delegations from the hall, followed by one delegate from Montana and two from South Dakota, with their state's senator B. F. Pettigrew. Four representatives from Nevada also retired. While the thirty-four bolters marched from the convention, the "regulars" cheered, booed, and shouted. The band tried to drown out the noise by a rendition of "Columbia, the Gem of the Ocean." Three Nevada delegates who remained in the convention were designated by the *Silver State* editor as "worse traitors to the state than Benedict Arnold." The Republicans nominated William McKinley without further opposition.

Henry Teller was the hero of the silver men. Fully redeemed from his earlier errors, he was the choice of the silver forces for the presidency. Twenty-seven Republicans declared their independence from the regular party and announced plans to obtain endorsements for Teller's candidacy from the Democrats, Populists, and the Bimetallic League.[12] Leaders in the new National Silver party also planned to support the Colorado senator.[13]

In addition to Henry Teller, a number of other men of national reputation were considered for the presidency on a ticket that would unite the silverites. Richard Bland was regarded by many as a leading candidate and apparently had a good chance to win the nomination. The important issue, however, was not which candidate the silverites nominated, but that they unify their forces. If they did not, said Senator Stewart, Marcus A. Hanna, the Ohio political boss, would be the next president of the United States.[14] The last was a reference to Hanna's strenuous campaign in favor of William McKinley for the Republican nomination.

When the Democrats met early in July, 1896, the convention was captured almost immediately by the silver men. The platform contained a declaration for silver coinage at 16 to 1 with gold. Lacking complete agreement on candidates, however, the Democrats favored Bland for the first three ballots, with William Jennings Bryan trailing. In the end, the Nebraska congressman's splendid oratorical ability, displayed in the famous "cross of gold" speech, won the delegates, and Bryan took the nomination. Arthur Sewall, a capitalist, but still a free-silver advocate, was chosen to run for vice-president.[15] The brave plans of the National Silver party organizers to put forward their own candidates were effectively destroyed by the Democrats' action in endorsing both free coinage and the nomination of William Jennings Bryan.

William Stewart was thus forced to accept the fact that he would not be a leader in a new national party devoted to silver. He wrote at the end of the Democratic convention that his observations at that assembly had convinced him that the silverite Democrats were sincere. It would, therefore, be a mistake for the Populists or the National Silver party to oppose them with another candidate. Furthermore, Stewart wrote, the platform was attractive to silver men and "radical enough for . . . me." Bryan was "more of a Populist than Democrat." The organizers of the National Silver party, Stewart said, had erred in failing to hold their convention first, but he, like others, had supposed that the Democrats would be controlled by "gold bugs." Concluding, Stewart advised that "we go to St. Louis and endorse the nominees of the Chicago Convention." There was no use in dividing the silver supporters by trying to name another candidate who would only duplicate Bryan's qualifications.[16] Stewart also advised his friends in Nevada to preserve the unity of the silver forces, and promised to "stump Nevada for the Chicago nominees."[17]

Having planned the St. Louis meeting, the silver men carried out their program. Francis G. Newlands was temporary chairman of the convention when the National Silver party met on July 22, 1896. His speech at that time followed the customary outline of such orations, denouncing the demonetization of silver, assuring listeners that the Silvermen only wanted the traditional money of the country restored for the purpose of expanding the circulating medium and raising prices, and asserting that true prosperity would return only through adoption of silverite programs.[18] The Democratic nominees, William Jennings Bryan and Arthur Sewall, received the endorsement of the National Silver party.

The People's party also met in St. Louis on July 22. The leaders of the drive for unity of all silver forces tried valiantly to convince the Populists that they should endorse the Chicago ticket. Bryan easily received the nomination for president. William Stewart seconded a nomination for Sewall for vice-president, but the supporters of the loyal, old-line Populist, Thomas E. Watson, won the post for their man. Sewall's capitalist background would never gain Populist allegiance.[19]

As the nation prepared for the election of 1896, eight national parties had presented candidates for the presidency. Three of the parties—the Democrats, the Populists, and the National Silver party—had nominated William Jennings Bryan, but the People's party had refused to support the vice-presidential nominees of the other two. Two separate Prohibition parties asked aid in doing away with strong drink. The Labor-Socialist party bid for votes on the left. Two gold-standard parties had offered candidates: the Republicans, with William McKinley, and the so-called National Democratic party, which splintered away from the regular Democrats in the dispute over coinage. The latter group nominated Senator John M. Palmer of Illinois for president at a convention boycotted by Nevada, Idaho, Utah, and Wyoming.[20]

Surrounding William Jennings Bryan was a disparate group with roots deep in the nation's political past. Bryan himself symbolized these interests. The son of a moralistic, Bible-reading, rural family who enjoyed participating at evangelistic revival meetings, he almost typified the American agrarian ideal. The ethical beliefs the Nebraskan absorbed as a young man, combined with the environment, made Bryan a true champion of the underprivileged, although he remained relatively conservative in his approach to problems. His identification with the so-called common people and his intense political ambition led to associations with others of similar interest.[21]

By 1896, furthermore, the weakening of the conservative forces in the Democratic party stemming from Grover Cleveland's devotion to hard money had brought forward a clamorous group which also exemplified the humanitarian impulse. The work of these persons for reform of the economic system was aimed at relieving the plight of workers and farmers whose financial burdens during the depression of the 1890s were especially critical. Some of the leaders were famous characters of American political history in their own right, including "Sockless" Jerry Simpson, Mary Elizabeth Lease, "Pitchfork" Ben Tillman, and other old Populists.[22] The rural orientation of the Populists, radicals, and their leaders led to their support of programs to reform patterns of land ownership, the management of transportation and communications systems, and the nation's financial structure.[23] Because of their common identification with, and devotion to, the supposed victims of deflationary economic policies and hard money, Bryan rather easily led the proponents of the crusade for inflation and soft money—that is, for free silver.

In Nevada, meanwhile, the political season started early with preparations for conventions. In 1896, moreover, the planners were increasingly charged with the responsibility for achieving what politicians referred to as "fusion." This movement began with an invitation from the Silver party of Nevada to supporters of the cause to join in a united effort.[24] Early in August, George Nixon, in a long editorial, wrote that Nevada had always led silverite political thought in the nation, and urged that it continue to do so. He encouraged the state's politicians to pursue fusion, or unification, of the three silverite parties to assure victory for bimetallism.[25] It seemed by midsummer, however, that the Silver party was having difficulties in maintaining its hold on some segments of the organization. A Republican antagonist reported a rumor that the Silvermen were foundering because Black Wallace had been out of the state for some months. Then the railroad lobbyist returned and apparently had matters under control.[26]

The problem almost certainly lay in the beginning of a power struggle for control of the Silver party. Nixon tried to reassure his readers that all was well within the party, but observers realized that the peripatetic Wallace was visiting several key towns of the state on what appeared to be an important errand. Finally, the several factions met near the end of August to effect some kind of compromise. Prominent in the discussions were George Nixon and William E. Sharon, representing Francis G. Newlands' supporters, and Black Wallace and W. A. Massey, friends of William Stewart. Others who arrived to talk and work out agreements represented the Populists and the Democrats. The chiefs of both latter groups were persuaded, with difficulty, to present a united aspect.[27] The members of the People's party later defected, but the Democrats held to their pledges in a move that worked to their advantage.

On August 29, 1896, the Democratic state central committee passed and publicized an amazing resolution. Saying that free coinage was the most important issue in the coming campaign, the Democrats "cheerfully" abandoned their political prerogatives to the Silvermen. They said they planned to nominate only presidential electors in order to maintain their legal status as a party. The resolution requested Democrats and their supporters to vote for "candidates representing the opposition to the gold plutocracy party of the nation and the state." The Democratic chiefs then bound themselves to adhere to any arrangements made by their "fusion committee."[28]

Two days later, Silvermen and Democrats met in Virginia City, where they had a "harmonious and enthusiastic" discussion in preparation for the state conventions then only a little more than a week away.[29] When the Silver party's convention assembled then in Elko on September 9, it must have been somewhat surprising to hear Thomas Wren, in making the keynote address, score both Democrats and Republicans for their adherence to the gold standard. The delegates adopted a motion to inaugurate discussions with the Democrats and Populists on fusion of the three parties' electoral tickets, but when the question of naming presidential electors arose, the division within the party became quite clear.

There was never a possibility of effecting a fusion between the Nevada Silvermen and Republicans after the national Republican party flatly declared in favor of the gold standard in 1896. Thenceforth, former Republicans in the Silver party had either to ally themselves with the Democrats who *did* support free silver, or abandon their convictions and rejoin the party of gold. Among those for whom the decision was especially painful was Thomas Wren; around him the battle began in 1896.

The fusionists—the Democrats and Silvermen—proposed to nominate Wren as a presidential elector. Wren declined the nomination, saying that he was a silver *Republican,* and that he did not choose "to be shoved into the Democratic party without leave or license." He accused various powerful Silvermen of attempting to disorganize the Silver party in order to elect Democrats, who would supposedly be more compliant to the demands of special interests. Supporting this view was Dr. Henry Bergstein of Reno, who claimed that he had been approached by an agent of the Southern Pacific railroad with a plan to disband the Silver party. Leaders of the fusionist faction pointed out realistically that the job of the party was to win votes for silver and to stay in office. The debate lasted for more than two hours in a "battle royal" that one sympathetic observer declared was "sure to leave scars on the Silver party that [would] be a long time in healing." The fusionists were described as having "scored a glorious victory," although the two factions fought constantly throughout the balance of the convention.

The Democrats also met at the same time in Elko and were likewise taken over by the fusionists. The delegates nominated only presidential electors. In a conciliatory move, one of the nominees resigned the nomination, leaving the vacancy that was offered to Wren. When Wren refused, the place was filled by B. F. Leete of Reno. The Democrats then concurred in the nomination of Francis G. Newlands for Congress. The Democrats offered no candidates of their own, although the ballot designated all the fusion men as Silver-Democrats. The electors were instructed to vote for

Thomas E. Watson for vice-president if the Bryan-Sewall ticket should be defeated nationally.

The platform of the fusionists pledged support to William Jennings Bryan and Arthur Sewall and endorsed the aims of the National Silver party. The statement declared "the restoration of silver to the place accorded it as a money metal by the founders of the Government to be the paramount issue." The joint parties endorsed the candidacy of John Percival Jones for United States senator and applauded the work of Congressman Newlands.[30]

The Populists had rebuffed the fusionists when they held their convention in Reno a few days preceding the Elko gathering. The main topic of debate was the proposed merger with the other silver parties, but the antifusionists won the argument after two hours of wrangling. The People's party then nominated presidential electors and a full slate of nominees for other offices, the most notable of which was that of James Doughty for Congress. The platform called the financial question "paramount," and endorsed the standard Populist reforms.[31]

When the Republicans met in convention a few days later, the members must have realized that they could no longer endorse free silver and maintain their connection with the national party. Nevertheless, the delegates supported the free coinage of silver at 16 to 1 with gold *by international agreement,* which apparently did not violate their affiliations with the national Republican party, and endorsed the nominations of William McKinley and Garret Hobart for president and vice-president of the United States. Other planks in the platform pledged the party's faith to the high tariff and endorsed the "purity of elections" law. The GOP nominated a full slate of candidates to make

William Morris Stewart

Francis G. Newlands

Charles C. "Black" Wallace

George S. Nixon

Samuel Post Davis

Reinhold Sadler

John Edward Jones   Thomas Wren

George William Cassidy

John Percival Jones

Newlands' reception when he returned to the House of Representatives after his treachery to Stewart.

Newlands: Well, boys, I'll tell you, I'm a staunch Democrat when drunk, and a rank Republican when sober, hi, hi, hi."

The pro-Stewart *Carson Morning Appeal* published these cartoons during the 1898–1899 election campaign.

William A. Gillespie

J. A. Denton

Earl W. Tremont

A. J. McGowan

Henry A. Comins

Frank Paul

Hirsch Harris

Trenmor Coffin

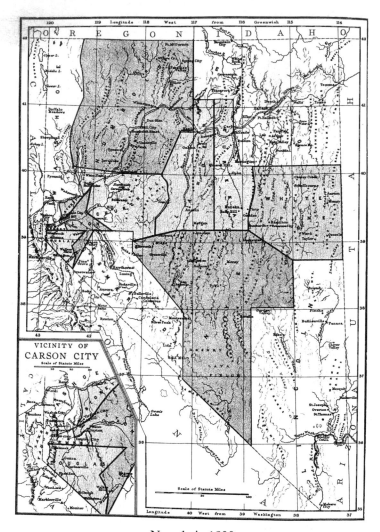

Nevada in 1890

what they probably apprehended would be a pointless race. The leading editor of the Republican press in Nevada, himself a nominee for presidential elector, wrote of the convention: "The Republicans . . . did good work. The utmost harmony prevailed. . . . Possibly it may not make a winning campaign, but the Silver Party of Nevada will know that there has been an election after the votes are counted."[32]

The campaign that fall was as colorful and noisy as any that had gone before, and the Silver-Democrats were confident of winning. Their confidence did not preclude a strenuous canvass, however. The *Silver State* printed nearly every one of Bryan's campaign speeches verbatim through the summer and autumn. Various partisan paraphernalia included "Bryan hats"—gray "stovepipes" with silver bands, or soft gray fedoras with small silver cords—and McKinley shirts with pictures of the nominee and the slogan "Sound Money and Protection" printed on the hard front.[33] Charges and countercharges followed each other with the usual regularity. In Elko County, the editor of the *Independent* approvingly reported that a local citizen, an off-reservation Shoshone Indian, had named his newborn son William Jennings Bryan Owyhee.[34] Nevadans on the Bryan speaking circuit of the Middle West and South were Senators Jones and Stewart, Francis G. Newlands, and Clarence D. Van Duzer.[35]

Near the end of the canvass, a writer for the *San Francisco Examiner* assessed the probable outcome of the Nevada election. Reporting that half the state's counties had no Republican ticket at all, the *Examiner* writer opined that John P. Jones was "sure of reelection to the Senate," while Francis G. Newlands had "good assurance of being returned to Washington."[36] Even the first scattering of returns showed that the California commentator had been too mild in his prediction. The Silvermen or Silver-Democrats carried every county except Douglas by large majorities. In no case did the silverites fail to win a majority of votes over their Republican and Populist opponents in the statewide contests. All the Republican and People's party presidential electors combined failed to capture as many votes as any one of the Silver-Democratic electors.[37]

The national tally, while promising on the surface, held mixed news for the silverites. In 1892, the Republicans had taken the electoral ballots of Washington, Montana, Wyoming, South Dakota, Nebraska, Minnesota, and Iowa; Oregon, California, and North Dakota divided their electoral votes; Nevada, Idaho, Colorado, and Kansas voted Populist; and Utah, Arizona, New Mexico, Texas, Missouri, Arkansas, Louisiana, and the Indian Territory (Oklahoma) all voted Democratic. In 1896, the only western states the GOP took were Oregon, North Dakota, Minnesota, and Iowa; and the California electoral vote divided eight Republican to one Democratic. All the other states west of the Mississippi River gave their electoral votes to Bryan. The popular vote for the allied silver parties in 1896, however, was less than it had been when they were separate four years before; in 1892, the Populists and the Democrats divided 6,595,285 ballots, but in 1896, the number had slipped to a combined vote for Bryan of 6,511,073.[38] It seemed that the silverite capture of the Democrats had decreased that party's effectiveness and contributed to an East-West rupture that would be difficult to repair. The westerners, with a smaller population and electoral vote, would need to work diligently to convince the East that free silver could bring economic benefits. In Nevada, however, silver was more than economics and more than a cause; Silver was the party in control of the state's political and governmental processes.

In the days before the Seventeenth Amendment, a state election was not completed until the legislature had made its choice for United States senator. In 1897, John P. Jones's term was expiring. As a candidate for reelection, he had no apparent opposition, although many persons regarded the senior senator as an interloper in state politics because he made no pretense of maintaining a bona fide residence in Nevada. Then, only a few days before the legislature would meet, George Nixon surprised almost everyone in the state by announcing that he would be a candidate for United States senator. Recovering from their shock, a few newspaper editors began to discuss the so-called home rule issue, pointing out Senator Jones's obvious dereliction. However, the general reaction to Nixon's announcement was disbelief, or even worse, hilarity. A man of quite small stature and only thirty-six years old, Nixon probably appeared somewhat ludicrous when compared to the more portly and mature senior senator.

It was obvious to some observers, however, that the announcement by Nixon indicated the continuance of the struggle for state control that had begun the preceding summer. William Stewart supported Senator Jones and the status quo, realizing that any threat to the established order was a menace to his own position. Stewart's friend, Hirsch Harris, wrote early in January, 1897, that Senator Jones believed that Francis Newlands was behind Nixon's bid. Harris was disturbed by the further fact that certain newspapers had given countenance to the home rule question, which the senator's supporters would rather have buried, realizing that Stewart was vulnerable on that count, too.[39]

Nixon's attempt was disposed of almost too quickly. Following the party caucus in the legislature, Henry M. Yerington wrote to Stewart: "On counting noses yesterday the Jones people felt assured of a good sized majority . . . therefore it looks as if little Nixon's bold move to capture the U.S. Govt. flash'd in the pan. . . ." Yerington hopefully concluded: "To an onlooker this stupid fiasco of little Nixon's simply assures the speedy and final break up of the so called Silver party . . . it was on its last legs anyhow so the quicker it goes under the better."[40]

On January 19, the Jones supporters won a decisive vote, thirty-five for Jones to three for Nixon. Reflecting Jones's defection from the GOP in 1894, the disgruntled Republicans attempted to mount opposition but the effort failed, due in large measure to the very small number of Republicans in the legislature.[41] To the public view, apparently Nixon's announcement had been only chimerical.

That the Nixon-Newlands combination had lightly undertaken their action was not true, however. What had taken place was rather clearly told in a letter from Black Wallace to Senator Stewart later in January:

The fight is over and Jones is elected and I want to say right here that it was your right hand friends enabled him to get there. Nixon made an ass of himself. . . . He was prompted behind the scenes by Newlands. Their break only resulting in killing Nixon off and crippling Newlands. If it wasn't for the personality of Sharon [William E. Sharon, Newlands's campaign manager], Newlands would go to the wall. . . . I think after reviewing the situation their making the break they did will result in an advantage to you.

Wallace warned his friend that Henry Yerington had allied himself with the Newlands combination and was directly involved in some of the congressman's activities.[42] The growing situation was hinted at in a letter to Stewart from an informant in Carson City who wrote that Nixon's "fizzle" had created an interesting "set of bedfellows."[43] Stewart, the completely professional politician, knew by that time that trouble portended for the time two years hence when he would himself be a candidate for reelection. He wrote cautiously to Wallace that he was "sorry that there [had] been any friction in Nevada over the Senatorial election. . . ." He added that he hoped it had "not created ill feeling which will give trouble in the future." Preparing for that future, the senator added, "Please send me a list of the members of the Nevada legislature making a check on the Senators who are holdovers."[44]

Even without the senatorial election, the legislature was embroiled in its own problems. The Silver party had a good working majority and might have expected to accomplish something constructive. In the senate, the eleven Silvermen easily outnumbered the three Republicans and one Democrat. The thirty-member assembly seated only two Republicans and one Democrat, the balance being Silvermen.[45] The main topics suggested for legislative action were woman suffrage, a revision of the state's mining laws, various ways of reducing expenses, and numberless local issues.[46]

Acting Governor Sadler addressed the session on the opening day. He paid a graceful tribute to Governor John Edward Jones, who had died in San Francisco the preceding April. Sadler then proceeded to outline the financial straits of the state, calling attention to the $7.5 million decline in assessed valuation of properties in the state since 1891. He asked remedy for the situation whereby the small property holders paid the major portion of the taxes, hinting that larger corporations had simply refused to pay their levies. Since 90 cents per $100 of assessed valuation (the current state rate) was insufficient to operate state institutions, Sadler said that other revenue would have to be found "unless there is a material increase in the assessed valuation of property." The executive suggested reinstituting the state board of equalization.[47]

Sadler declared that it was for the legislators to decide whether certain appropriations should be increased or reduced for the biennium. He expressed his dissatisfaction with the condition of the state's mining industry and said the demonetization of silver had "effectually depopulated many villages once inhabited by industrious and prosperous people, and deprived farmers in the contiguous valleys of a home market." He held out some hope that gold mining in the state would soon help to improve the economy. One suggestion was that the legislature might memorialize Congress to participate in a program of reclamation of arid lands to the end that people might thus be encouraged to colonize in the state. However, he made no other suggestion for state action on this important problem. Concluding, Sadler charged the legislators to observe "the most rigid economy" and suggested that they find some ways of reducing state expenses without further cuts in the salaries of state employees.[48] (Sadler himself had had cause to rue the previous session's action in eliminating the lieutenant governor's salary. After an attorney general's opinion that no vacancy existed in the lieutenant governor's office, the acting governor had to sue the state to collect a salary for his work in the governor's office.)

The legislators of the eighteenth session produced a book of *Statutes of Nevada* somewhat smaller than that of the preceding session. Apparently to obviate the necessity for making an extremely slim volume, they caused to be printed in the same covers with the *Statutes* the complete texts of the Nevada and United States constitutions, together with an index for each. The financial difficulties were not solved; the tax rate remained at 90 cents per $100 of assessed valuation, and the enactment of a poll tax as a prerequisite for registration to vote could not have been expected to produce large amounts of revenue. The lawmakers, thus rejecting a chance to enact responsible fiscal legislation, turned instead to tourism for solution to the crisis.[49]

Assembly Bill 8 was a proposal calling for the licensing of prizefights in the state. The editor of the *Nevada State Journal* commented when the bill was introduced, "Its passage would be of great advantage to the state." He wrote that a high fee would keep "travelling pugs" out of Nevada, bringing in a "better class" of fighters. In addition, he pointed out, newspaper reporters and imported audiences would bring added money to local service businesses. The *Journal* editor assured his readers that both Bob Fitzsimmons and Jim Corbett would gladly give an exhibition in Nevada under the proposed conditions.[50] Designated the "glove contest" bill, AB 8 was generally expected to pass in the legislature, although important opposition came from persons who condemned gambling or brutality.[51]

The proposal passed, and the *Nevada State Journal*'s legislative observer wrote that Nevada would now have "slugging matches as a source of revenue for the State." The *San Francisco Post* editor sarcastically commented that Nevada was the ideal place for legalized brutality: "The air of the mountains is bracing, the location is far from the madding crowd, there is no chance for the contagion of immorality to spread, the distance is too great for reformers to get there. . . ."[52]

The governor's office reported receiving sixteen pieces of mail favoring the new law to one against. Governor Sadler explained in a telegram to the *New York Journal* that he had signed the bill because the people of the state favored it. He said there were no constitutional grounds for vetoing the proposal, even if he had wanted to do so. The high license fee, he continued, would prohibit "fake fights." Furthermore, Sadler felt that the sport was no more "dangerous to life and limb than football games."[53] Negotiations began immediately for the match between Corbett and Fitzsimmons.

In the ensuing several weeks, the people of the state paid a great deal more attention to their first attempt to bring tourists to Nevada than they did to politics. Nearly everyone who lived at the state capital, where the bout took place, saw the fighters in training on the roads around the city and made a personal choice for the championship. One young observer decided that Fitzsimmons was more friendly than Corbett, who was somewhat of a dandy and was nicknamed "Handsome Jim."[54] An unhappy critic wrote that Carson City was "filled with pimps, gamblers, cutthroats, pickpockets, and hobos of all kinds."[55] When the fight had finished, with Fitzsimmons victorious in the fourteenth round, Senator Stewart wrote to a friend in Nevada in a somewhat defensive tone: "The prize fight in Nevada has made our state rather notorious during the past few months. I am glad it was a square fight and that no disorder occurred. Some of the good religious people in the East who worship gold and hate humanity have made it the occasion for some assaults on me."[56]

The legislature did not end its session until several weeks after enacting the prizefight bill. Unfinished business included the constitutional amendment for woman suffrage, then pending its required second passage. One of the first resolutions of the senate provided for the change. Early in the session, Mrs. Frances Williamson addressed an evening meeting of the state senate in support of the cause.[57] She established headquarters in Carson City and directed her force of women, and workers all over the state circulated petitions for presentation to the lawmakers. But when the legislators voted on the suffrage amendment, they defeated it and by parliamentary maneuvers shut off a chance for reconsideration. One supporter in the assembly challenged an opponent to a rough-and-tumble settlement of the contest, but cooler spirits prevailed. The women expressed their disappointment and resolved to redouble their efforts.[58]

As the eighteenth session of the Nevada legislature closed on the fifty-fifth day, observers generally agreed that the term had been less than auspicious. One of the strongest Silverite editors in the state wrote simply that the session had been "clean" and that most of the bills were of local interest only. He summarized: "While those who composed the eighteenth session . . . were not, perhaps, as brilliant as some who have figured in former Legislatures, they were, on the whole, men of average intelligence and appeared to legislate for what they believed to be the best interests of the state."[59]

The opposition press was not so friendly. The *Reno Evening Gazette*'s editor claimed that the lawmakers had spent their time in "small talk," and were men "too ignorant to compose a ten-word sentence grammatically."[60] The *Gazette* writer was somewhat more defensive about the eighteenth session when criticism came from outside the state. In response to articles in the national press attacking Nevada's morality in legalizing prizefights, the editor wrote, "It makes us sick to read as much rot about Nevada, when every other State in the Union is doing worse."[61] Another observer sat in Washington and assessed the meeting. William Stewart wrote to Black Wallace: "I congratulate you upon your very successful management of affairs in Nevada during the last legislature, but that is an old thing. You have been a success for so long that everybody seems to take it for granted that you will make a success of everything you undertake."[62]

The McKinley prosperity meanwhile began to affect the West. A senator in the Nevada legislature had draped his desk in mourning on inauguration day, feeling that times could only get worse,[63] but the economy of the region showed a definite improvement. Livestock prices increased markedly; the water situation seemed favorable; and gold mining seemed to promise some rewards.[64] Despite this prosperous aspect produced ostensibly by his opponent, when William Jennings Bryan made a western speaking tour in the summer of 1897, the circuit of the defeated candidate seemed like a victory parade.

Huge crowds greeted the "silver-tongued orator" as he crossed the western states. In Nevada, the train had barely passed the state line from Utah when the local politicians began to board the cars to shake Bryan's hand. The western political hero made brief talks at several stopping places across the state: at Wells, he gave residents "a few words of cheer"; at Deeth, "all the people of the town were at the depot"; at Elko, his thirty-minute speech was "enthusiastically applauded . . . [by] all the town"; at Carlin, he made "a few apt remarks" in the town library; at Battle Mountain, he was "heralded by the firing of bombs and the glad shouts of the entire populace"; at Winnemucca, a reported one thousand persons greeted him with "the firing of cannon, bursting of bombs, and the sweet strains of music"; at Reno, "an immense crowd" came to hear a short speech at 2:30 in the morning.[65] The tour continued into California, where Bryan met "cheering thousands" in Sacramento, Stockton, and Fresno.[66]

Enthusiasm and crowds of people could not change political facts, however. The silver issue appeared moribund. Even the *Silver Knight-Watchman,* a silverite paper of which William Stewart was the chief sponsor, was in financial trouble that only large infusions of cash could alleviate.[67] And Stewart constantly lost his battles to maintain support for the state's federal institutions. Each time an appropriation was proposed, it took all the power he could muster to keep the Carson City mint open.[68] The senator's former supporters even had to be reminded that he still controlled a certain amount of patronage, and that he would not tolerate willful attacks.[69]

To all public appearances, at least, the Silver party of Nevada had now been so thoroughly merged with the Democratic party that it would never again be an entity of itself. The depression was apparently nearly ended, for everyone could see that the economic situation had improved even though the betterment was only slight. The state had experienced the first heady contact with a horde of tourists and expected more. Who needed the Silver party?

The answer was that the politicians needed the Silver

party—all the men who had entered the arena for the first time and found the experience interesting or profitable, all the new office holders who attained their places under the Silver label and wished to keep their posts. Most of all, the railroad needed a vehicle for maintaining its hold on the state. A United States senator would be elected at the next legislative session, and the Central Pacific's men had found the Silvermen supinely agreeable for three terms. Therefore, if the silver issue was nearly dead, a way would be found to revive it.

NOTES

¹ *Silver State,* November 7, 1895, p. 2; November 8, 1895, p. 2.

² *New York Times,* December 18, 1895, p. 7. The western Republicans in the Senate generally favored free silver; a loose alliance with the Populists was therefore logical. In the House of Representatives, the Democrats were silverites.

³ *Silver State,* April 16, 1896, p. 3.

⁴ *Ibid.,* April 20, 1896, p. 3.

⁵ W. H. Wheelock, Chagrin Falls, Ohio, to William Stewart, June 29, 1896. Stewart papers.

⁶ William Stewart to George Nixon, March 3, 1896. Stewart papers.

⁷ The Bimetallic Union, to which the Nevadans had previously given their support, was operated in 1896 almost as a personal office of the president, A. J. Warner. William Stewart and Marion Butler, senator from North Carolina, were both members of the executive board of the Union, and both constantly complained to Warner that he was usurping too much power and spending too much money without proper authorization. See letters in Stewart papers, February to April, 1896.

⁸ William Stewart to John D. Thorne, Panacea, North Carolina, May 11, 1896; Stewart to George Rutledge Gibson, February 12, 1896. Stewart papers.

⁹ William Stewart to R. C. Chambers, Salt Lake City, February 4, 1896. Stewart papers.

[10] William Stewart to C. C. Wallace, March 2, 1896. Stewart papers.

[11] *Silver State,* July 17, 1896, p. 2.

[12] *New York Times,* June 19, 1896, pp. 1 and 7; June 20, 1896, p. 2; see also *Silver State,* June 18 to June 21, 1896, *passim.*

[13] William Stewart to J. J. Mott, June 25, 1896; Stewart to William H. Porter, Santa Rosa, California, July 2, 1896. Stewart papers.

[14] *Silver State,* June 23, 1896, p. 3.

[15] William Jennings Bryan, *First Battle: A Story of the Campaign of 1896* (Chicago: W. B. Conkey Company, 1896), pp. 210–218.

[16] William Stewart to Marion Butler, July 14, 1896. Stewart papers.

[17] William Stewart to C. A. Norcross, Reno, July 28, 1896. Stewart papers.

[18] Draft in Newlands papers.

[19] Bryan, *First Battle,* pp. 238–279.

[20] *Reno Evening Gazette,* September 2, 1896, p. 1; *Silver State,* September 15, 1896, p. 3.

[21] Paul W. Glad, *The Trumpet Soundeth,* (Lincoln: University of Nebraska Press, 1960), pp. 1–34.

[22] J. Rogers Hollingsworth, *The Whirligig of Politics* (Chicago: University of Chicago Press, 1963), pp. 32–33.

[23] Glad, pp. 51–52.

[24] *Silver State,* June 22, 1896, p. 2.

[25] *Ibid.,* August 6, 1896, p. 2.

[26] *Reno Evening Gazette,* August 19, 1896, p. 3.

[27] *Ibid.,* August 24, 1896, p. 1.

[28] *Silver State,* September 2, 1896, p. 3.

[29] *Ibid.,* August 31, 1896, p. 3.

[30] *Weekly Independent* (Elko, Nevada), September 13, 1896, p. 2; *Reno Evening Gazette,* September 9, 1896, p. 3; September 28, 1896, p. 3.

[31] *Silver State,* September 7, 1896, p. 3.

[32] *Reno Evening Gazette,* September 11, 1896, pp. 2–3.

[33] *Silver State,* July 31, 1896, p. 3.

[34] *Weekly Independent,* September 21, 1896, p. 2.

[35] *Silver State,* August 20, 1896, pp. 2–3.

[36] *San Francisco Examiner,* November 1, 1896, p. 24.

[37] *Reno Evening Gazette,* December 15, 1896, p. 4; Nevada, Secretary of State, *Political History of Nevada, 1965,* p. 186.

[38] Bryan, *First Battle,* pp. 607–611.

[39] Hirsch Harris to William Stewart, January 12, 1897. Stewart papers.

[40] H. M. Yerington to William Stewart, January 18, 1897. Stewart papers.

[41] *Nevada State Journal,* January 19 and January 20, 1897, *passim.*

[42] C. C. Wallace to William Stewart, January 28, 1897. Stewart papers.

[43] P. B. Ellis to William Stewart, January 30, 1897. Stewart papers.

[44] William Stewart to C. C. Wallace, February 9, 1897. Stewart papers.

[45] *Nevada State Journal,* January 16, 1897, p. 4; January 20, 1897, p. 2.

[46] *Ibid.,* January 20, 1897, p. 3.

[47] Nevada, State Legislature, *Appendix to the Journals of the Senate and Assembly,* Eighteenth Session (1897). Governor Sadler's message. The State Board of Equalization had had an interesting history. An attempt to relieve local officials of railroad pressure came with the enactment of a law creating the board in 1891. The act made a state prerogative of assessing railroad property (although in practice this meant that county assessors made the valuations and the corporation acceded to, or appealed, the decisions). The brief tenure of the board produced some dramatic results. Total assessed valuation rose by over six million dollars between 1890 and 1892, and revenues increased some $67,000 in the same period. In 1893, the board was abolished through the activities of the railroad lobby. Subsequently, personal property taxes rose, and railroad taxes decreased in the reversion to the old local-assessment plan. See James G. Scrugham, *Nevada,* I, 364–365. Note that the years of increased revenue from railroads are the same as those cited above, chapter III, n. 66.

[48] Nevada, State Legislature, *Appendix to the Journals of the Senate and Assembly,* (1897). Governor Sadler's message.

[49] Nevada, State Legislature, *Statutes of Nevada,* Eighteenth Session (1897), chapter II, p. 12.

[50] *Nevada State Journal,* January 26, 1897, p. 3.

[51] *Ibid.,* January 28, 1897, p. 2.

[52] *Ibid.,* January 29 and 30, 1897, *passim.*

[53] *Ibid.,* January 31, 1897, p. 3.

[54] Lucy Davis Crowell, "One Hundred Years at Nevada's Capital," typescript of an oral history interview, conducted by Mary Ellen Glass for the Oral History Project of the Center for Western North American Studies, University of Nevada, 1965, p. 54.

[55] *Silver State,* March 15, 1897, p. 3.

[56] William Stewart to Alexander McCone, March 25, 1897. Stewart papers.

[57] *Nevada State Journal,* January 29, 1897, p. 2; February 3, 1897, p. 3.

[58] *Ibid.,* February 17, 1897, p. 3.

[59] *Ibid.,* March 14, 1897, p. 2.

[60] *Reno Evening Gazette,* March 10, 1897, p. 2.

[61] *Ibid.,* March 17, 1897, p. 2.

[62] William Stewart to C. C. Wallace, March 27, 1897. Stewart papers.

[63] *Reno Evening Gazette,* March 9, 1897, p. 2.

[64] *Ibid.,* March through June, 1897, *passim.* See Appendix I.

[65] *Silver State,* July 3, 1897, p. 3.

[66] *Ibid.,* July 6, 1897, p. 3.

[67] William Stewart to I. N. Stevens, Denver, Colorado; Stewart to Dennis Sheedy, Denver; Stewart to Henry Rives, Salt Lake City, Utah; all December 7, 1897. Stewart papers.

[68] William Stewart to H. M. Yerington, March 6, 1897; Stewart to Jewett W. Adams, March 10, 1897. Stewart papers.

[69] Sam Davis of the *Appeal* had made a few telling thrusts at the junior senator in his paper during the late winter of 1897. A friend wrote to Stewart, "I had a talk with Wallace last night and he told me he would notify Samuel that if he wished help in matters of his own he had better not wilfully attack the friend of the people he expected aid from." P. B. Ellis to William Stewart, February 6, 1897. Stewart papers.

VI

The Election of 1898≠1899

REINHOLD SADLER'S conduct as acting governor of Nevada was determinedly honest and ruggedly individualistic. In the course of his work in the office, he received dozens of inquiring letters from homeseekers all over the nation and replied by sending information about the state's lands which were open for homesteaders or colonizers. In the effort to create an atmosphere of receptiveness to new settlement, the acting governor continually appointed delegates to various conventions where the theme was the opening of new acreages.[1] On the other hand, Sadler showed little interest in similar projects for promoting mining and failed to appoint state representatives to the 1897 International Gold Mining Convention on the excuse that he could find no one "who would promise to attend."[2] Early in 1898, when a controversy erupted concerning the transportation across the state of cattle from California districts infected with "tick fever," the acting governor stood firmly with the Nevada cattlemen in refusing to allow diseased animals in the state—this, despite the reported offer of a $100,000 bribe from certain livestock interests.[3] A fair amount of the executive's time was consumed in answering questions from representatives of the national press concerning Nevadans' views of the conflict that became the Spanish-American War. Sadler put the people of his state on the side of the Cuban belligerents.[4]

With all of his other activities of business and politics, however, Reinhold Sadler never forgot that he represented the Silver party and the cause it symbolized. Inevitably, in speaking of his state's problems, he blamed the "silver crime" and always declared his own loyalty to the cause of the white metal, even when this posture became quite hopeless politically.[5] By 1898, Sadler's views on most public questions were a matter of record, a record upon which he felt that he could be a candidate for governor of Nevada. He accordingly announced his plans and proceeded to pursue the office.

Along with the governor's post, all other state offices were subject to new elections; several men sought the congressional seat, and a United States senator would be elected as William Stewart's term expired. The race for the Senate was the topic of many conversations, beginning as early as February, 1898. At mid-month, George Nixon wrote to Francis Newlands, outlining his objections to the congressman's desire for the upper-house seat. The divisions within the Silver party were clearly evident in Nixon's discussion. C. C. Wallace, Nixon wrote, had " 'fixed' about all the papers and many of the principal wire pullers" in the state in favor of William Stewart's candidacy for reelection. Nixon advised his friend to postpone a race for the Senate until John P. Jones could be retired in 1902. He further urged Newlands at all costs to avoid bitterness between himself and Senator Stewart and to shun any antagonism of Black Wallace. Nixon believed that a challenge to Stewart in 1898 would split the party. If Newlands, instead of himself, had sought the Senate seat in 1897, Nixon thought, the two could have overcome Wallace's machinations; but in February, 1898, it was too late.[6]

Newlands had tried to "fix" a few "wire pullers" himself. He hired William F. Herrin, the railroad attorney, to take charge of the affairs of the Sharon estate for a somewhat inflated fee. However, Herrin was also beholden to Stewart for many earlier favors. He therefore assumed an aspect of neutrality.[7]

As the season wore on, prices of commodities seemed to be rising, although mining remained depressed. Then an early spring drought nearly erased expectations for a good yield of crops, and hopes for real recovery fell. Early in the year, William Stewart issued his pamphlet *Analysis of the Functions of Money,*[8] to demonstrate his continued loyalty to the silver question. Sam Davis greeted the publication with the observation, "I don't know whether many people will read your book on the functions of money as the drouth is making times so hard that most have about settled down to the idea that we will never have any acquaintance with the article or its function."[9]

About the middle of July, with political conventions in the near future, some silverites in the old parties, along with the Silvermen, began to discuss a new Silver-Democratic fusion. The idea met favor in some quarters, but the Republicans objected as they had before, explaining that they could vote for Silver candidates without doing violence to their principles, but that they could not participate in a fused Silver-Democratic party. Many Republicans had joined the Silver party solely in the interests of bimetallism; they had no intentions of becoming Democrats by devious means. They announced, therefore, that they would be forced to secede from a Silver-Democratic fusion, and warned that such a move would weaken their own and Silverite positions.[10] The Republicans, however, were never a majority or even a very large fraction of the Silver party, and thus their partisan councils were generally ignored or considered only lightly. The discussion of fusion with the Democrats continued, and Republicans everywhere were called enemies of free silver.[11] The Republicans were, moreover, so demoralized that some observers thought they might not present a slate of candidates for the fall elections. Even the Democrats had a better chance of electing their ticket.[12]

As the maneuvering for a merger of Democrats and Silvermen continued, it became increasingly clear to some observers that the issue of free silver had assumed a secondary place in a search for political positions. In arguing this point, Sam Davis warned that failure to join the silver-supporting parties would show the enemies of the white metal that "we have placed the prospective spoils of office above the principle." The Republicans would win, Davis cautioned, and worst of all, the country at large would have evidence that Nevada had given up the silver cause for local political preferment.[13] It did seem that the Silver party was the only guarantor for the politically ambitious. Men of most political convictions had discovered this, but the Nevada press—the first leader of the cause—became disillusioned. Many of the editors who had so warmly supported the state's third party began to fall away in the summer of 1898, or at least to support individual office seekers instead of the party as a whole.

By September, topics of political conversation were mainly the possibilities of fusion and the chance that Francis G. Newlands might oppose William Stewart's bid for reelection. The first was rather quickly disposed of; the second created a division in state politics that persisted for several decades.

The Democrats held the season's first state convention the second week in September. The question of fusion agitated the delegates considerably, with the men from the western part of the state in favor and those from the eastern counties opposed. The first serious quarrel showed the strength of the various forces. A dispute erupted over the seating of the Humboldt County delegation (which would support fusion). Ten "duly accredited delegates" from the northern county were ejected from the hall on the grounds that there were no Democrats in Humboldt County.[14] A near riot ensued. Then a resolution to appoint a committee to work with the Silvermen to effect a merger failed by three votes. On reconsideration, it was decided to await action from the Silver party.[15]

The Silvermen convened the next day. Busy in the preconvention activities were supporters of Francis G. Newlands (mainly George Nixon and Will Sharon) and partisans of William Stewart (C. C. Wallace and Hirsch Harris). Newlands let it be known that he would like to be endorsed for senator, bypassing Stewart. Stewart's men were too strong, however, and threatened the congressman with failure even to be renominated for the House if he persisted. The two factions finally agreed that if Stewart's men failed to be elected to the legislature, Newlands was free of obligation to support the senator.[16] Hirsch Harris meanwhile worked to have the party endorse Stewart's candidacy by declaration in the platform.[17]

The question of top state posts was also quickly disposed of. Before the Silvermen met, four candidates had announced their desire to be nominated for governor.[18] Sadler's men did their work well, however, and he was selected by the caucus as the party's nominee. The Silver caucus also chose a slate of candidates for other offices which left open the positions of state controller and superintendent of public instruction, both to be offered to the Democrats on a fusion ticket.

The next day, September 9, the Silver committee on fusion met with a counterpart from the Democrats. The Silvermen offered, in addition to the posts of controller and superintendent of public instruction, the candidacies for lieutenant governor and one regent of the state university. The Democrats rejected the offer, in spite of all efforts by the Silvermen. Francis Newlands entertained the party chiefs at his home during part of the discussions, but even open-handed hospitality failed to change the Democrats' position.

The Silvermen then nominated a full slate in a vote recorded as unanimous, including Francis G. Newlands for Congress, Reinhold Sadler for governor, Sam Davis for controller, and several others. The main part of the platform reaffirmed dedication to bimetallism and coinage of the white metal at 16 to 1 with gold. The Silvermen adopted several other planks which revealed intraparty issues: "We earnestly recommend the re-election of William M. Stewart to the Senate of the United States, and pledge the Silver party . . . and the nominees of this convention to his support for that office." Nevada could "not afford to lose

[Francis G. Newlands] as her representative in . . . Congress." Railroad debts should be collected, and the ICC strengthened. The platform also saluted Newlands's efforts to obtain passage of reclamation bills in the Congress and expressed "profound appreciation" to Senator Stewart for "tireless efforts" in the state's behalf.[19]

Despite the apparent harmony in these brave declarations, however, the Silvermen were severely divided at almost every level. Sam Davis's nomination for state controller, for example, came through the party's passing over the incumbent, C. A. LaGrave. LaGrave had been in elective county and state offices for twenty years and was much distressed by the slight he received from his fellow politicians. He circulated a petition to secure a place on the ballot as an Independent, in opposition to Davis.[20]

Meanwhile, the Democrats adopted a platform that endorsed "every line, word and syllable" of the 1896 Democratic national platform and claimed that theirs was "the only silver party in the nation." The statement argued that the Silver party of Nevada was "detrimental to the silver interest" and existed only to give political office to a few men. The Democrats were not completely united, however. Their nominees for state offices included neither an attorney general nor a congressman.[21] Francis G. Newlands would apparently have no Democratic opposition and would run under the Silver label. Later, the Democratic state central committee endorsed Newlands and he was designated a Silver-Democrat on the ballot. The party at the congressman's home thus bore some fruit.

When the Republicans met in Reno a few days later, divisive forces were at work. The band arrived at the appointed time and began to play the usual patriotic airs. No delegates appeared in the hall. Someone dismissed the musicians, asking them to come back in an hour. When the convention finally assembled, observers knew that agreement would be difficult.[22] During the deliberations, the ubiquitous Black Wallace received a strongly worded note from William Stewart: "Mr. Yerington tells me that you are interfering with the Republican Convention to get a strong man to run against Newlands. He is very much annoyed at the rumor. . . . I know you will do nothing of the kind, but I write to let you know what is said and warn you against the appearance of evil."[23] Stewart apparently thought that Newlands's reelection to Congress was insurance against a fight for the Senate seat. Wallace probably did not agree, but he did abandon the search for a Republican congressional candidate, no doubt in the interest of mollifying Yerington. The latter could sometimes be useful, and it would be pointless to antagonize him needlessly.

When the Republicans began to make their nominations, they found that they were unable to agree upon a man for the Congress. The caucus had failed to make a decision, unable to compromise their need for a silver supporter and their desire for political office. C. C. Wallace and party members who were committed to the candidacy of Dr. W. H. Patterson, a regular Republican, were thus ignored. Patterson, angered by the turn of events, walked out of the convention after addressing an apathetic gathering on his loyalty to Republican principles—that is, the gold standard. The sparsely attended assemblage then adopted a platform. The financial plank reiterated the party's "faith and devotion to the great Republican principles of bimetallism, protection, and reciprocity." The "final adjustment of the money question" would be made by the Republican party, the Nevadans asserted. The GOP offered the candidacy of William McMillan of Storey County for governor, and nominees for most other posts except congressman.[24] The Newlands-Nixon-Yerington combination had managed, then, to assure Newlands a chance at high office with almost no opposition. The Silvermen had conferred the nomination; the Democrats had refused to oppose the congressman, and Yerington's action had reduced Republican strength. While motives for these activities varied, the result was the same.

The Populists, like the Democrats, had refused all attempts to merge their organization with other silverites. They nominated Thomas Wren for Congress and presented candidates for most other state offices. The major theme of the convention and the platform was condemnation of the railroad.[25] Black Wallace, rebuffed by the Republicans and under stress to protect Senator Stewart's position, turned to covert support of Wren for Congress. This, despite their previous disagreements over the railroad's position in Nevada politics, dating at least from the 1894 dispute on the Reilly funding resolution. Newlands later charged that Wren had received generous assistance from Wallace and Stewart in both money and campaign materials.[26]

That the campaign that fall was extremely confusing to the voters is demonstrated by the election returns. Reinhold Sadler waged a sturdy fight against three opponents. His supporters called Sadler friendly, generous, and honest; his opponents said he was a drunkard and a consorter with questionable characters.[27] The governor won his election in a ballot so close (twenty-two votes) that the Republican McMillan demanded a statewide recount. The Newlands-Wren contest, while bitter, was relatively ineffective on Wren's part. Newlands's majority over Wren was 2,655 in

8,877 votes cast. The Republicans took only one major office, that of superintendent of public instruction. Silvermen were elected to every other state post. Except for the congressional race, however, in only one case (a supreme court justice) was the Silver party plurality for a state office larger than 1,316; in many races, the plurality was only a few hundred. Wherever three or more men contested a post, not one won a majority.

The election of 1898 showed a loss of power for the Silvermen, with the results directly traceable to the earlier split in the party. The major portion of party funds that year was used by Stewart in support of his own reelection plans. Legislative candidates who were weak received additional help if they agreed to vote for the senator. This process touched all the rest of the ticket. Reinhold Sadler was probably the most severely affected by the trading; his near defeat was the result of failing to carry the state's largest county (Washoe) by a fair margin. Sam Davis was also a victim, winning the race for state controller by just over 400 votes in 9,701 cast.[28] To make matters worse, newspapers in the East and Middle West reported William Stewart's defeat, saying that he had failed to carry the necessary number of legislators into office.[29]

The senator had perhaps not carried enough lawmakers on his ticket, but the fact that the battle was not yet over was indicated in a letter a few days after the election from William H. Mills, a high official of the Central Pacific. Mills wrote: "If in the situation of things there is a place where I may be of service to you at any time, do not fail to apprize me of it. I am more than willing to perform any service I may be able to render in your interest."[30]

Francis G. Newlands, on the other hand, apparently was satisfied that he had fulfilled any obligations he had to Senator Stewart. The congressman thereupon announced his plan to seek the Senate seat. He had considered declaring his intentions before the party conventions, Newlands said, but had been prevented from doing so because he was too ill to make the necessary trip to visit state political supporters. The Silver convention had nominated him then for Congress, and in the interests of party harmony, he had accepted. Then the Silvermen had divided during the election canvass between Stewart and anti-Stewart factions. As Newlands read the returns, the anti-Stewart group had won, and no one was obliged to support the senator further. The congressman reported that such an arrangement had been consummated between the two campaign managers, Will Sharon and Black Wallace. He then claimed that he had been scrupulous in observing the agreement and accused William Stewart and C. C. Wallace of conspiring to defeat him by supporting Thomas Wren for Congress.[31]

Newlands's announcement was almost a literal bombshell to his supporters and opponents alike. From newspaper offices all over the state came editorials denouncing him for treachery to Stewart or praising his forthrightness and honesty. No person who was interested and active in state politics was indifferent. The long-awaited crisis in Nevada's political life had arrived. This culmination stemmed, however, not from the most recent campaign, but from the similar division in 1897. In the background were also the ambitions and desires both of individuals and of corporations. The roots of the controversy were both intricate and interesting.

After their defeat in 1897 in the Nixon-Jones contest for the Senate seat, Newlands and Nixon probably planned to use at another time the experience thus gained. Certainly their amateurish performance had given them little but experience. Black Wallace had written to Stewart shortly after the 1897 debacle, "I think as you do that Newlands is an ass pure and simple[;] divest him of his money and he wouldn't rank above a dry goods clerk."[32] In spite of powerful opposition and the contemptuous attitudes of his fellows, however, Newlands now believed he could make the race for the Senate, knowing that he also had powerful support. Months before the election, early in June, 1898, Will Sharon had written a long letter to the congressman, discussing the possibility of a contest with William Stewart. Sharon reported then that he had spoken to A. C. Cleveland and had found that politician in favor of Newlands's candidacy. Indeed, Cleveland was so anxious for Stewart to be defeated, Sharon wrote, that he (Cleveland) would make the race himself if Newlands did not. Sharon had refused to urge his relative to try to unseat Senator Stewart, however, saying, "I am not so sure. You know best whether or not you can afford to tackle Stewart." Henry Yerington, on the other hand, was not so cautious. His message to Newlands through Sharon was that he would support any election activity the congressman chose to undertake.[33]

Newlands replied to Sharon's and Yerington's communications, saying that he felt that Stewart's usefulness was at an end. Stewart's habit of talking at length against people who differed with him had "intensified enmities and alienated friendships." Before he made a final decision, Newlands wrote that he would tour Nevada attempting to assess voters' opinions. Astutely, the congressman had realized that silver would soon decline as a campaign issue. A visit with the voters might develop new questions, allowing him thus to deal from a position of strength instead of from the weakness of a worn-out slogan.[34]

The plans and schemes of the Newlands faction of the Silver party were no secret to William Stewart and his friends. The same month that Nixon and Newlands were assessing their chances, Black Wallace wrote to the senator warning that Newlands and A. C. Cleveland might oppose Stewart's reelection. Wallace had admonished his friend, "Make your financial arrangements East so we will not be caught with our breeches down." He had also reminded Stewart to secure John W. Mackay's promise of support, for Cleveland was then claiming the old miner's endorsement.[35] Shortly before the state conventions, William F. Herrin, in reflection of his arrangements with both sides, had written a similar warning and suggested a compromise. Herrin thought then that a suitable Silver ticket would present Abner C. Cleveland for governor, Francis G. Newlands for congressman, and support for William Stewart's reelection to the Senate. Newlands, said Herrin, was anxious to have Cleveland in the statehouse because Cleveland as governor would appoint the congressman to the Senate if a vacancy occurred.[36] No such assurances could be obtained from Reinhold Sadler, since he and Newlands were not on good terms.

Throughout the summer of 1898, preceding the party conventions, Stewart had received perhaps a dozen letters from various cronies in Nevada, warning of a possible challenge from the Newlands group and urging him to return to the state as soon as possible.[37] Ordinary campaigning would not suffice. One Stewart man, who had reported

Newlands's making "unwarranted and slanderous" remarks about the senator, had offered to obtain extra help from Miller and Lux, an interstate cattle-ranching business.[38] Other support had come from party leaders and Stewart's colleagues in the Senate. The latter sent letters to the newspapers of the state, praising his efforts for Nevada and the nation.[39] Certainly, Stewart needed every champion he could find. One of his correspondents of the summer located a source of public apathy in the senator's association with "that damned old Huntington." This friendship with the railroad magnate was regarded as a "rebuff" by certain Silvermen.[40] By the end of the summer of 1898, Stewart's candidacy was clearly in trouble. A worker in Virginia City wired the senator soon after the party conventions, "You had better come up today and attend to legislative ticket if you don't wish to be beaten."[41]

The Silver party's fall campaign had opened then during the first week in October with a rally in the main street of Carson City. William Stewart and Francis Newlands had appeared together on the platform, and both had declared their loyalty to the party and its cause.[42] The next week, Abner Cleveland had announced that he would oppose Stewart for the Senate and had begun to canvass the state in his own behalf. Cleveland complained that Stewart was not a bona fide resident of the state, and even resorted to bad verse to prove his point: "[Stewart] will holler for silver and Southern Pacific and make noise like a ram, But for the interest of Nevada he don't care a damn." Other stanzas of the rhymes accused Stewart of fathering the "Crime of '73" and of various moral derelictions.[43] As the campaign progressed, it seemed clear to some observers that Cleveland was a stalking horse from some other unnamed politician.

His own aspirations were not taken seriously, especially after his flight into verse.[44]

In October, shortly before the election, a Washoe County political ally wrote to Stewart's private secretary that the enemy was surely Francis Newlands. But the senator's friends could not decide what to do: name Newlands as an opponent? ignore the problem? try to split Newlands's vote in some way? distribute derogatory material?[45] Newlands himself had attempted to allay the rumors until after the election. As the canvass was drawing to a close, the congressman spoke at Virginia City. There, he had delivered a speech very complimentary to his supposed opponent, saying that the senator was true to the cause of free silver. Regarding allegations of Stewart's hypocrisy on this issue, Newlands had said: "I indignantly resent these charges and challenge any man to point to a single instance in Senator Stewart's career when his whole energies were not devoted to the silver cause."[46]

Nevertheless, overt opposition to Stewart had developed during the campaign. Henry Yerington, the manager of the Virginia and Truckee railroad, the major owner of the Republican *Territorial Enterprise,* a Newlands supporter, and a political dilettante, had used his influence openly against his former friend. Recognizing this antagonism from a key source, Sam Davis—then a Stewart supporter—had arraigned Yerington for his company's practices of charging even higher rates than the Central Pacific. The V & T, Davis declared, charged such high fees that it was more profitable for shippers to haul their goods several miles to the Central Pacific platforms than to send freight by the nearby V & T. Furthermore, Davis asserted that the V & T evaded its just taxes and debts in the state.[47] The political competition between the two railroad companies was thus bared.

Throughout the fall campaign, pressures had arisen, too, for additional financing for individual legislative candidates. At one point, Reinhold Sadler had importuned Senator Stewart to supplement the Silver party's campaign chest, indicating that the electoral situation was desperate and that Congressman Newlands had refused such a request.[48] Other solicitations had come from individuals and newspaper owners for payments of various sums in return for "influence." Often, these offers merely reflected the hard times of the mining camps.[49] One politician wrote before the election that Stewart's supposedly-pledged assembly candidates had demanded money for their support of the senator's reelection. These, wrote Stewart's informant, were "worrying the life out of me."[50]

By election time, the senator's unfavorable situation had brought realization that additional money would be needed. A Humboldt and Lander County mining man wrote to Stewart: "If I knew where C. C. was would call him. . . . If I had some funds to use would go to Austin, Kennedy, & Cortez & Beowawe before election. I think a thousand could be well used in good hands."[51] A Douglas County worker wrote in the same vein to Stewart's secretary: "Please remind the Senator to send me $42. he knows. . . . You should also send me a little to work around with election day. There are five men I want to see and *fix*."[52]

Then the votes for legislators were counted, and the *Morning Appeal* had claimed the election for William Stewart's ticket, while most of the other newspaper writers had declared that the senator had failed to elect his men. A former state senator wrote to Stewart that the election in Storey County had been an example of corrupt practices through the activities of "Newlands Sharon & Co." He asserted that the Newlands faction had engaged in "perfidy . . . the infamy of which they can never shake off."[53]

Only nominal amounts had been spent in the election to that point. Stewart kept careful account of the sums he paid from his personal funds on a sheaf of paper: two columns of figures, with amounts of from $5 to $100 paid to various workers with the same amount still owing.[54] The Silver party central committee claimed to have collected $1,150, and spent just $1,000.[55] The campaign for the Senate thus entered an entirely new phase, beginning with Newlands's announcement on December 6.

With a different situation now confronting them following Newlands's challenge, Black Wallace wrote to William Stewart with advice on the conduct of the contest. He suggested having the chairman of the Democratic national committee, Senator James K. Jones of Arkansas, write to Democratic leaders in Nevada requesting their support for Stewart's reelection. Wallace did not, however, intend to rely solely upon political favors. He appended a postscript to his letter, "Dig up 40,000 if you can get it."[56] The Newlands forces also engaged in money raising to the extent that one of the congressman's supporters bragged openly that he "had the money to buy the necessary votes and could pay three dollars" to one spent by the Stewart party.[57]

Francis Newlands himself apparently believed that there was no need to bribe the legislators directly. He offered personally to pay the expense of about $35,000 for a state-

wide referendum on the election question. His detractors
flung the accusation that the congressman was actually
trying to buy a state election at Senator Stewart's expense.[58]
The offer, at any rate, was ignored, and the candidates
continued to solicit support from legislators and the press.

At mid-December, William Stewart was still receiving
scattered offers of aid from various parts of Nevada. W. N.
MacNamara of Virginia City wrote to the senator, "My
services at your command." As MacNamara assessed the
situation, Newlands was only a tool of the "Sharon crowd,"
and actually felt no hostility to Stewart's reelection. Nevertheless, the Comstocker presented his credentials: a prison
term already served for "bribery and corruption" in California in a situation similar to the one confronting the
Nevada senator.[59] Another worker wrote that he was help-
ing to spread the slogan "Newlands treachery" with some
effect, and was circulating a petition for presentation to the
legislature. The slogan failed to serve Stewart with some
of the important newspapers; the *Nevada State Journal,*
the *Carson News,* the *Silver State,* the *Gardnerville Record,*
and the *Yerington Rustler* all declared independence from
his cause.[60]

Finally, at year's end, the two combatants arrived in the
state capital, in preparation for the opening of the legislature. Stewart, reported to be "full of fight," established his
headquarters in a $100-a-day suite at the Ormsby House.
Newlands took similar rooms at the Arlington Hotel, where
he was described as "in good health and spirits," and prepared to "put up a lively battle."[61] After the customary
amenities in celebration of the New Year (libations of
"bimetallic eggnog," "senatorial punch," or "gubernatorial
punch," depending upon which gathering one attended),

the state capital settled in for a vigorous and deadly-serious struggle. The newspapermen, having the strongest weapons, fired the first salvos.

The *Morning Appeal,* now with Sam Davis's stepson, Henry Mighels, as editor, hired Charles Kappler, William Stewart's erstwhile private secretary, for editorial and writing chores. The sheet then became a campaign organ for the senator's reelection. Francis Newlands, supposed at one time to have said, "Anything to beat Stewart," was thereupon designated "Anything Newlands" by the *Appeal.* The congressman was lampooned in cartoons and attacked in dozens of articles under that sobriquet. A series of letters and articles published over the name of Thomas Wren scored Newlands unmercifully. He was labeled weak, vacillating, ambitious, vain, cowardly, and traitorous.[62]

The *Nevada State Journal* gave its columns to Francis G. Newlands. In that paper, Stewart, having supposedly failed to secure enough votes to assure his reelection, was characterized as a desperate, "wretched old man," who now proposed to terrorize the lawmakers into giving him a new term. He had imported "a gang of professional gun and knife fighters" who would intimidate legislators "weak and cowardly enough" to be swayed from their commitments. The *Journal* named as Stewart's unsavory coterie C. C. Wallace, Stephen Gage, "Colonel" Jack Chinn, Will Virgin, and Dave Neagle.

Wallace, of course, was well known in Nevada politics. Gage had once held the same position Wallace now held with the railroad and had been transferred to California. There, he had gained the appellation "the king of lobbyists." Gage's presence in Nevada was regarded as a new demonstration of the railroad's interest in Stewart's fortunes.

Chinn was a Kentuckian and a former "famous race horse man." As an employee now of the Central Pacific, he was said to be prepared to "give the fractious legislator anything he wants from an argument to a fist or gun fight." Chinn had represented railroad interests before the Kentucky legislature. Neagle was famous in western criminal and political history as the reputed "gun for hire" killer of Judge David Terry. Will Virgin was a member of a pioneer Carson Valley family and was said to be Gage's protégé.[63] Virgin acquired a job as an attaché with the legislature.

The presence of Chinn and Neagle became a cause célèbre of the campaign. Neagle was an especially unsavory character, a fact that no Stewart supporter could obscure. In attempting to do so, however, the *Appeal* writers clouded the issue still further. In an editorial on January 8, 1899, the paper's scribe attempted to hand Neagle over to the Newlands forces:

Since when has Nagel [*sic*] not been working in the interest of Mr. Newlands? Does Newlands call Nagel a cold-blooded murderer because he killed Judge Terry? Has Nagel ceased to be in the employ of Newlands . . .?

A lenient public never charged that Newlands was the direct beneficiary of Judge Terry's death. All suspicion was kept down that Newlands had in any way connived at bringing about a meeting between Judge Field and Judge Terry. Nagel was present with his gun ready and Terry was shot down, and the Sharon estate was relieved from a most embarrassing position.[64]

The innuendos in this piece were never clarified by any writer, although they were widely resented. Francis Newlands had indeed had an early conflict with David Terry when he supported Stephen Field as a candidate for president over Terry's opposition in 1884. The conflict continued when it appeared that Sarah Hill had married Newlands's father-in-law, Senator William Sharon. In 1885, when William Sharon died, his heirs, including Francis Newlands, fought bitterly with the supposed widow for the estate. The opposing attorneys were David Terry, for Mrs. Sharon, and, among others for the Sharon estate, William M. Stewart. After several years of litigation, Stephen Field, sitting as a judge in an appeals court, ruled against Sarah Sharon (by then Mrs. Terry) and the attorney. Subsequently, in 1889, Field and Terry met in a California restaurant; Field was accompanied by Dave Neagle. An argument ensued, and Neagle shot Terry. Neagle and Field were both charged with murder, and both were freed. Sarah Hill Sharon Terry was driven mad by this series of events, and later died in a California insane asylum.[65] Presumably, then, the occurrence could have been interpreted as relieving the Sharon estate "from a most embarrassing position," since it removed both of the Terrys from contention with the Sharon heirs. The embarrassment of Dave Neagle's presence in Carson City in 1899, however, accrued to William Stewart and his allies, not to Francis Newlands. Nonetheless, the *Appeal* pursued the Newlands connection with the Terry killing through January.

The other newspapers of the state began to evince concern over the peculiar crowd of people who had rallied to William Stewart's support. The editor of the *Carson News* suggested organizing a vigilance committee to protect the decent citizens of the town. The *Reno Evening Gazette* and the *Nevada State Journal* abandoned their traditional feud to condemn the importation of hired gunmen to influence a local election. The nation's newswriters also became very much interested in the Nevada contest, printing a

variety of versions and opinions. A cartoon in the *San Francisco Examiner* depicted Stewart with his "body guards,"
framed with a gun and a knife. The *Appeal,* still attempting
to free the senator of the onus of bringing in hired toughs,
reported that Colonel Chinn was an official observer for
the Democratic national committee. When Senator Jones,
the chairman of the committee, denied the report in a telegram to Nevada Democrats, Newlands supporters had a
brief and gleeful celebration.[66]

The good humor of the Newlands forces was short-lived,
for this faction was in deep difficulties. On January 12, the
Silver party central committee convened in Carson City.
Black Wallace announced that he held proxies from members all over the state and appeared to believe that he had
the situation completely in his hands. Only fifteen of the
fifty-one members of the committee actually attended; the
rest had been induced to give proxies. The first order of
business was the introduction, by the Stewart-Wallace
group, of a resolution calling for the resignation of Will
Sharon as chairman of the central committee; the charge
was that he had opposed Stewart's reelection contrary to the
platform's pledge. Sharon's friends protested so strongly that
the matter was postponed for a week. Also tabled was a
resolution condemning Francis G. Newlands "for his bad
faith in the campaign, for his act of treachery in breaking
the pledge of the Silver party platform, for his covert
opposition to his own party ticket." The Stewart-Wallace
members of the committee further proposed to denounce
the congressman as "a traitor to his party, an enemy to the
silver cause and a dangerous man to society."[67]

Their victory in tabling the motions was regarded by
Newlands men as a sign that the railroad, or Stewart, fac-

tion was weak and would fail to organize the legislature. Senator Stewart never admitted any such weakness. In an interview following the meeting, he called the Newlands-Sharon men "damned cowards and a pack of ingrates," and continued with several stronger terms characterized by a listener as "profanity, obscenity and billingsgate."[68]

The day before the central committee reconvened, Francis Newlands addressed a rally in Carson City. In a two-hour speech, he accused Stewart's forces of having "packed" the central committee against his own candidacy. He declared that he welcomed William Stewart's ill will and regarded the senator's disapproval as a "badge of honor." At the same time, Newlands attacked the Central Pacific–Southern Pacific combine for corrupt control of Nevada and California politics, comparing the corporation's activities to those of the notorious railroad companies in New York and Pennsylvania. Newlands illustrated his argument by citing the railroad's Nevada profits: $3,000 per mile per year after taxes. Furthermore, he said, in spite of the fact that the road was capitalized at $60,000 per mile, the company paid taxes in Nevada on an assessed valuation of $10,000 or $11,000 per mile. The congressman begged his listeners to help destroy this unfair burden and restore integrity to the lawmaking and elective process.[69]

When the Silver party central committee met again on January 19, forty-four members were present or represented by proxy. The first order of business was the introduction by H. A. Comins of a resolution condemning William Stewart as "dangerous to society," commending Francis Newlands, and excoriating the railroad. The resolution was tabled, thirty-one votes to thirteen. A second proposed resolution declared the meeting illegal and its purpose "unbecoming." The resolution lost by the same vote as Comins's, thirty-one to thirteen. C. M. Sain of Lovelock then introduced the Stewart faction's resolution censuring Francis G. Newlands. After opposing speeches by George Nixon and Comins, the resolution passed, thirty-one votes to thirteen. A demand for Will Sharon's resignation gained approval by the same tally.

Will Sharon used the time allotted him for a statement of his group's position. He excused his own refusal to continue in support of William Stewart by saying that he "considered it no part of his duty to jam down the throats of the majority of the people of this State a man whom they had absolutely repudiated." He accused Stewart and Wallace of acting illegally, and declared them guilty of betraying the party and the party's aims. Continuing his defense, Sharon alleged that, for the railroad faction, devotion to silver was "a mere cloak for their nefarious designs." Stewart, he asserted, had "never yet cast an honest vote for silver," and the senator's "only warm supporter" was the representative of the railroad. Wallace, in turn, Sharon claimed, was only the slave of the "arch gold-bug of them all," Collis P. Huntington.[70] Words could not change the result; Sharon, Newlands, and their supporters left the meeting, outcasts of their party. The Stewart-Wallace group had acquired enough proxies and had convinced a sufficient number of the central committee members to ensure the outcome.

The state's press voiced the full spectrum of opinion on the central committee's action. The *Morning Appeal* called the decision "the most positive and radical action ever taken in politics in this State," and argued for a complete reorganization of the Silver party into a disciplined organization.[71] The *Nevada State Journal* gave the story a black headline, "Treachery Profound," and censured the Stewart-Wallace combine.[72] The contentiousness in the press and public finally reached an impasse as the legislature opened in an atmosphere of extreme tension.

The amount of money available for a single legislator's vote was reported in various sums up to $5,000. William Stewart had presumably been able to "dig up 40,000," while Francis Newlands—before his defeat in the central committee—was described as prepared to spend $150,-000.[73] The wife of a Stewart worker in Reno found a valise full of money in a closet and knew that this was a Stewart "sack."[74] The editor of the *Nevada State Journal* recognized the vital issues as he wrote on the day of the senatorial election: "Today the two branches of the Legislature will cast their votes for United States Senator. . . . The honor of the State is trembling in the balance. It means either freedom, self government and an honorable future, or continual slavery to a soulless corporation, with all of the untold evils and humiliation of political bondage. God save the commonwealth of Nevada."[75]

The presession caucus for the nineteenth session had been chaotic as the two major groups labored to control their delegates. The Stewart men won the privilege of naming the officers; the skirmish was over and the Newlands supporters near defeat. Senator H. A. Comins, the highly respected representative of White Pine County, reflected on the events in a statement to a reporter for the *Nevada State Journal.* Discussing the organization of the legislature and the events in the Silver party central committee, Comins said he believed that the people of the state supported his attempt to condemn the railroad lobby and to name William Stewart "an enemy of the State" for his subservience to the corporation's interests.[76] The voters would not, however, have an opportunity to express their thoughts.

.The day before the actual voting in the senatorial election, a test vote in a parliamentary maneuver had indicated that a tie could result; the Stewart men counted fourteen certain ballots in the assembly; the anti-Stewart men, the same number. One man was absent and one refused to be counted, but observers believed that these votes would divide.[77] Less than a majority vote in the lower house would force the legislature into a joint convention with each vote counted equally. The more numerous assembly therefore held the balance of power.

The balloting took place on the ninth day of the legislative session, January 24, 1899. William Stewart was formally nominated in the state senate by Adolph Livingston of Ormsby County, and the nomination was duly seconded. Abner C. Cleveland, Warren Williams of Churchill County, and P. L. Flanigan of Washoe all received nominations. No other names were presented. Stewart received nine votes; his opponents divided six. The proceedings in the senate occupied just twenty-four minutes.[78]

The assembly held a very stormy session in the afternoon the same day. When the clerk called the roll, Assemblyman W. A. Gillespie of Storey County failed to respond. After a search, the sergeant-at-arms announced that he could not find the missing representative. Parliamentary moves to delay the proceedings failed. Finally, A. J. McGowan of Ormsby spoke, nominating William Stewart for United States senator, calling the candidate "a fearless advocate" for free silver, a man "true to party principles and party pledges." McGowan declared that "the name of Nevada would be disgraced" if Stewart's reelection failed, and that Nevada would be "dead" if Stewart were not in the Senate to keep the silver question before the country. W. J. Henley of Esmeralda and Earl Tremont of Eureka also made seconding speeches, praising the senator's "tireless energy" and declaring that the future of the state was at stake. A. C. Cleveland also received a nomination. A few other courtesy nominations were made and the voting began. Francis G. Newlands, realizing that he had been completely out-maneuvered, refused to allow his name to be presented. A defeat at that time could only harm his plans for the future. William Stewart thus received fifteen votes, a majority of those present, with Gillespie still absent.

The next afternoon, a joint session of the two houses formally declared Stewart elected and technically the matter was finished. However, Gillespie's absence and widespread charges of corruption caused the lawmakers to impanel a special assembly investigating committee to seek the basis of the accusations. Earl W. Tremont was appointed chairman of the group. Only Assemblyman Gillespie and one other member were specifically involved in the charges, but nearly all of Senator Stewart's supporters were suspected or covertly accused of various corrupt practices.

The day after the investigation began, Tremont reported that one of the men had been exonerated. Gillespie's absence remained a matter of comment. When Tremont's committee decided that the charges were unfounded, only one committeeman dissented.[79] Many people whispered "whitewash." The matter of the election and the allegations of criminal activity were closed by the legislators, but not by the press and public. The Silver party had been sundered by the actions of the past few days; the topic could thus not be passed over lightly.

W. A. Gillespie, the absentee assemblyman, received a great deal of adverse publicity. In a statement to newsmen, the representative explained his absence from the legislature by saying that he had not been chosen to support William Stewart and knew that a member of his own (Republican) party could not be elected. He therefore went home, and he declared that he had a right to do so. Nevertheless, it was widely believed that Gillespie had been paid to play truant.[80]

Sam Davis later told another version of Gillespie's defection. Davis, who should have been in a position to know, wrote that the assemblyman was actually kidnapped by Sam Jones (brother of John P. Jones) and held incommunicado at Jones's home in Empire. Gillespie received $1,800 for his two days' stay outside of Carson City, Davis reported.[81]

Other senators and assemblymen gained or lost reputations over the election incidents. A. J. McGowan, who had nominated William Stewart in the assembly, had vowed, only a week before the legislature opened, never to vote for the senator. Before the end of the legislative session, McGowan realized that he was finished with Nevada politics and announced that he would leave the state. An editor who had supported Francis Newlands wrote, "May the devil speed his departure from the State which he has disgraced."[82] Senator J. A. Denton of Lincoln County was pledged before the session opened to vote for A. C. Cleveland. Denton wrote to Cleveland and various newspapers afterward, explaining that he had voted for Stewart to avoid voting for Newlands. He admitted, however, that

Stewart would have won the election without his (Denton's) vote. The Lincoln County senator's reputation for probity was ruined by his actions and his weak explanations. Newspaper writers and others pointed out that Newlands's name was not presented to the legislature, while Denton had violated a solemn pledge to Cleveland.[83] Denton never served another term in the senate; he received one term in the assembly after several years had passed. By March, both Gillespie and McGowan were reported working for the railroad; Gillespie was in an office in Oakland, California, and McGowan was with the corporation's law department.[84] Earl Tremont, with Senator Stewart's sponsorship, received a position in the Bureau of the Census.[85]

The men who managed to stay clear of the taint of railroad influence received as much praise as their opponents received censure. Frank S. Gedney, the assemblyman from Elko, was a very young legislator, barely past twenty-one years of age in 1899. After the investigating committee's report, the young representative had suggested breaking a ten-gallon bottle of cologne on the speaker's table "to remove the stench of the day's proceedings."[86] His incorruptibility in voting against Stewart, along with that of the representatives of Douglas County, was widely reported.

E. D. Walti of Cortez, Nevada, wrote perhaps the most honest appraisal of the election. In a letter to Congressman Newlands, Walti said, "i wonted to see you go to the Senat in plase of Mr. W. Stewart but the Railroad is powerful. . . ." He told Newlands that his friend, Senator P. H. Hjul of Eureka County, "promised to vote for you but could not stand out against Black Wallis or the Railroadsack. . . . [*sic*]"[87] A more constructive comment came from another campaign worker who wrote to suggest that Newlands work to bring the Southern Pacific–Central Pacific under the control of the Interstate Commerce Commission. The achievement would make the representative "invincible before the people of this state. . . . Our people are ripe for this question of railroad domination," the writer concluded.[88] The people of Nevada showed that they were ready at least for a change in their legislature; only one senator and three assemblymen survived the next elections.[89]

The Nevada legislature was bought and paid for in 1899 by the railroad forces to assure William Stewart's reelection. Thus it was demonstrated again that the corporation would use any means including bribery and intimidation to elect a man who would be compliant to its needs. Only the strongest men could have stood against the pressure.

As the legislators prepared to settle other questions of state importance, they might have observed that other states had had similar experiences in electing United States senators. Many displayed in greater or lesser intensity the graft, bribery, and corruption that led to increasing demands for direct, popular election of senators. In fact, the situation became so acute in Delaware, California, Pennsylvania, and Utah, that the legislatures of those states adjourned without agreement, despite the command of the United States Constitution that they elect senators to represent their states.[90]

NOTES

[1] See Governor's Office Letter Box, 1897–1899. Nevada Historical Society.

[2] Sadler's notation on letter, International Gold Mining Conven-

tion to the Governor of Nevada, June 18, 1897. Governor's Office Letter Box, 1897–1899.

[3] Samuel Post Davis, ed., *The History of Nevada*, 2 vols. (Reno: The Elms Publishing Company, 1913., I, 436–437.

[4] Telegrams, *New York World* to Governor Sadler; Sadler to New York World [1896]. Governor's Office Letter Box, 1893–1898.

[5] *Reno Evening Gazette*, January 29, 1906, p. 1 (obituary). See also, Sadler's legislative messages in Nevada, State Legislature, *Appendix to the Journals of the Senate and Assembly* (1895–1903).

[6] George Nixon to Francis G. Newlands, February 19, 1898. Newlands papers.

[7] *San Francisco Examiner,* January 7, 1899, p. 12.

[8] William M. Stewart, *Analysis of the Functions of Money* (Washington, D.C.: William Ballantyne and Sons, 1898).

[9] Sam Davis to William Stewart, June 19, 1898. Stewart papers.

[10] *Morning Appeal,* July 20, 1898, p. 2.

[11] *Ibid.,* July 28, 1898, p. 2.

[12] Charles M. Sain to William Stewart, June 19, 1898; Sain to Stewart, June 21, 1898. Stewart papers.

[13] *Morning Appeal,* August 5, 1898, p. 2.

[14] The assertion that no Democrats voted in Humboldt County (Winnemucca) had some basis in fact. George Nixon, the political boss of the county, was a firm Silverman and tolerated little opposition.

[15] *Morning Appeal,* September 8 and September 9, 1898, *passim; Reno Evening Gazette,* September 8, 1898, p. 1.

[16] Francis G. Newlands to William F. Herrin [December, 1900]. Newlands papers. See also: *Morning Appeal,* January 4 and January 5, 1899, *passim.*

[17] The plan to have endorsement of William Stewart's reelection included in the party platform was outlined in a letter from Hirsch Harris to the senator. Harris concluded that such a move would "prevent a fight afterwards." Hirsch Harris to William Stewart, June 15, 1898. Stewart papers.

[18] *Morning Appeal,* August 27, 1898, p. 2; August 30, 1898, p. 2. The suggestion that Newlands would support A. C. Cleveland was in a letter, William F. Herrin to William Stewart, August 13, 1898. Stewart papers.

[19] *Reno Evening Gazette* and *Morning Appeal,* September 7 to September 10, 1898, *passim.*

[20] *Morning Appeal,* September 9 to September 16, 1898, *passim.*

[21] *Ibid.,* September 10, 1898, p. 3.

[22] *Ibid.,* September 17, 1898, p. 3.

[23] William Stewart to C. C. Wallace, September 14, 1898. Stewart papers.

[24] *Reno Evening Gazette,* September 16 and September 17, 1898, *passim; Morning Appeal,* September 17, 1898, p. 3. Stewart and Wallace later obtained for Patterson the superintendency of the state insane asylum.

[25] *Reno Evening Gazette,* September 12 and September 17, 1898, *passim.*

[26] Francis G. Newlands to William F. Herrin [December, 1900]. Newlands papers. The accusation that Stewart and Wallace had supported Thomas Wren for Congress was later repeated in several newspaper articles.

[27] *Morning Appeal,* October 9, 1898, p. 3; *Reno Evening Gazette,* October 25, 1898, pp. 2 and 3.

[28] Nevada, Secretary of State, *Political History of Nevada, 1965,* p. 186; *Nevada State Journal,* January 10, 1899, p. 2; January 17, 1899, p. 3.

[29] John L. Garber (Western Union Telegraph Company officer) to William Stewart, November 15, 1898. Stewart papers.

[30] William H. Mills to William Stewart, November 17, 1898. Stewart papers.

[31] *Morning Appeal,* December 6, 1898, p. 3.

[32] C. C. Wallace to William Stewart, February 16, 1897. Stewart papers.

[33] William E. Sharon to Francis G. Newlands, June 6, 1898. Newlands papers.

[34] Francis Newlands to William Sharon, June 26, 1898. Newlands papers.

[35] C. C. Wallace to William Stewart, June 20, 1898. Stewart papers.

[36] William F. Herrin to William Stewart, August 13, 1898. Stewart papers.

[37] See Stewart papers, May to July, 1898.

[38] Isaac Frohman to William Stewart, August 1, 1898. Stewart papers. Frohman was the attorney for Miller and Lux; he was also a former private secretary to Francis G. Newlands.

[39] *Morning Appeal,* August 14, August 18, August 19, 1898, *passim.*

[40] A. A. Proctor to William Stewart, August 8, 1898. Stewart papers.

[41] Matt Riehm to William Stewart, September 18, 1898. Stewart papers.

[42] *Morning Appeal,* October 5, 1898, p. 2.

[43] *Ibid.,* October 18, 1898, p. 3.

[44] *Ibid.,* October and November, 1898, *passim.*

[45] C. H. Norcross to Charles Kappler, October 24, 1898. Stewart papers.

[46] *Morning Appeal,* November 4, 1898, p. 3.

[47] *Ibid.,* October 23, October 25, 1898, *passim.*

[48] Reinhold Sadler to William Stewart, October 14, 1898. Stewart papers.

[49] Nate Roff to Charles Kappler, October 16, 1898. See also several other letters asking for money in return for political favors. Stewart papers.

[50] L. P. Wardle, Virginia City, to William Stewart, October 18, 1898. Stewart papers.

[51] J. A. Blossom to William Stewart, November 1, 1898. Stewart papers.

[52] George I. Lamy to Charles J. Kappler, November 4, 1898. Stewart papers. (Emphasis in text.)

[53] Edward D. Boyle to William Stewart, November 17, 1898. Stewart papers.

[54] The practice was to pay a voter a set sum to vote for the candidate, with the same amount paid again if the candidate was elected. See Effie M. Mack, "William Morris Stewart . . .," p. 100. Stewart's notes on election funds are in the Stewart papers.

[55] "Report of the State Auditing Committee of the Silver Party of Nevada, 1898." Nevada Historical Society.

[56] C. C. Wallace to William Stewart, December 4, 1898. Stewart papers.

[57] J. C. Hagerman to William Stewart, December 8, 1898. Stewart papers.

[58] *Morning Appeal,* December 13, 1898, p. 3.

[59] W. M. MacNamara to William Stewart, December 15, 1898. Stewart papers.

[60] Thomas J. Tennant to William Stewart, December 17, 1898; J. C. Hagerman to Stewart, December 16, 1898. Stewart papers.

[61] *Morning Appeal,* December 29, 1898, p. 3.

[62] *Ibid.,* January, 1899, *passim.*

[63] *Nevada State Journal,* January 1, 1899, pp. 2–3.

[64] *Morning Appeal,* January 8, 1899, p. 2.

[65] A. Russell Buchanan, *David S. Terry of California: Dueling Judge* (San Marino: The Huntington Library, 1956), pp. 199–231. See also, Carl Brent Swisher, *Stephen J. Field: Craftsman of the Law* (Washington, D.C.: The Brookings Institution, 1930), pp. 340–345.

[66] *Nevada State Journal,* January, 1899, *passim.* See especially issues of January 4, 7, 12, and 13. *San Francisco Examiner,* January 7, 1899, p. 12. See also, scrapbook, "Editorial Comment," in the Newlands papers.

[67] *Nevada State Journal* and *Morning Appeal,* January 13, 1899, *passim.*

[68] *Nevada State Journal,* January 14, 1899, p. 2.

[69] *Ibid.,* January 19, 1899, pp. 2–3.

[70] *Ibid.,* January 21, 1899, p. 3.

[71] *Morning Appeal,* January 21, 1899, p. 2.

[72] *Nevada State Journal,* January 20, 1899, p. 3.

[73] *Morning Appeal,* January 5, 1899, p. 2; *Nevada State Journal,* January 6, 1899, p. 2.

[74] Amy T. Gulling, "An Interview with Amy Gulling," typescript of an oral history interview, conducted by Mary Ellen Glass for the Oral History Project of the Center for Western North American Studies, University of Nevada, 1966, p. 75.

[75] *Nevada State Journal,* January 24, 1899, p. 2.

[76] *Ibid.,* January 17, 1899, p. 3.

[77] *Ibid.,* January 24, 1899, p. 3.

[78] Nevada, State Legislature, *Journal of the Senate,* Nineteenth Session (1899), pp. 25–26.

[79] Nevada, State Legislature, *Journal of the Assembly,* Nineteenth Session (1899), pp. 25–40.

[80] *Nevada State Journal,* January 28, 1899, p. 3.

[81] Samuel Post Davis, *The History of Nevada,* I, 432.

[82] *Nevada State Journal,* January 26, 1899, p. 2. See also, *Delamar Lode,* February 7, 1899, p. 1: "Lincoln County Dishonored."

[83] *Nevada State Journal,* February 28, 1899, p. 2.

[84] *Ibid.,* March 26, 1899, p. 2; March 31, 1899, p. 2.

[85] William Stewart to W. R. Merriman, Director of the Census, March 7, 1899; Earl Tremont to Stewart, April 2, 1900. Stewart papers.

[86] *Nevada State Journal,* February 5, 1899, p. 3.

[87] E. D. Walti to Francis G. Newlands, February 20, 1899. Newlands papers.

[88] F. M. Huffaker to Francis G. Newlands, February 6, 1899. Newlands papers. Newlands pursued the course that Huffaker advised. When he died, Senator Newlands had gained recognition as an outstanding worker for railroad regulation.

[89] Nevada, Secretary of State, *Political History of Nevada, 1965*, pp. 154–155.

[90] For accounts of the problems of senatorial elections in various states, see the *New York Times:* on Montana, January 21, 1899, p. 1; Utah, March 11, 1899, p. 2; California, March 20, 1899, p. 1; Delaware, March 28, 1899, p. 7; Pennsylvania, April 21, 1899, p. 1. For comment within Nevada on several of these, see *Nevada State Journal,* January 26, 1899, p. 2; March 16, 1899, p. 2.

VII

The Fusionists of 1900

THE LEGISLATURE of 1899 was so affected by the senatorial election and the subsequent criticism that the lawmakers were nearly unable to accomplish any constructive work. Governor Sadler's message reflected discouragement. He mentioned a state debt of more than $563,000, over half of which, he complained, was uncollectible. Furthermore, as a second reminder of the state's financial problems, the governor was forced to ask for deficiency appropriations for several state agencies. Sadler was certain (on the eve of Nevada's second great mining boom) that mining could never be a substantial source of income, and he suggested several ways of helping to spur an agricultural economy.[1]

Seventeen days of the session passed with no important bills introduced; only local problems engaged the attention of the legislators. Then Senator Comins of White Pine County introduced a resolution to memorialize Congress to amend the Constitution to provide for direct election of United States senators. The resolution passed unanimously, and Governor Sadler signed it a few days later. On the same day that the Comins resolution passed, A. J. Mc-Gowan introduced, and finally maneuvered to passage, a bill to repeal the "purity of elections" law.[2] The actions of the past few weeks were thus "legalized," retroactively. One more significant action provided the state with nominal direct election of senators. The law provided for placing the names of senatorial candidates on the regular election ballot, giving voters an opportunity to designate their choice. The act further prohibited payment of any money or reward to any elector in return for his vote.[3] While the legislature would still make the final selection (as provided by the United States Constitution), the lawmakers would be morally bound to elect the candidate with the largest number of popular votes. Other bills which would have required amelioration of railroad abuses or registration of lobbyists met death speedily. Nearly all other bills were only of local importance.[4]

Politics, meanwhile, could not be neglected. When the mint at Carson City was reduced to the status of an assay office early in the spring of 1899, Francis Newlands and his supporters said that Senator Stewart had been remiss in his duty; Stewart's friends said that if Newlands were truly as powerful as he claimed, the congressman would have managed to keep the mint operating.[5] George Nixon and Newlands exchanged letters agreeing to a plan to remake the public character of the *Silver State*. The sheet, which had pioneered the silver cause in Nevada and had been the most active partisan of the Silver party, would now claim to be independent. Fearing for his political life two years hence, John P. Jones spent more than his accustomed time in the state, and was reported on the Comstock campaigning against Newlands's supposed plan to take the Senate seat in 1902.[6] William Stewart continued to use his railroad friends, even to the extent of requesting that depots be placed where they would be inconvenient to his enemies.[7] The senator also gave up his interest in his newspaper, the *Silver Knight-Watchman,* selling it to a member of the Democratic national committee.[8] He thus gave a sign that he was contemplating abandonment of the silver cause to return to the Republican party.

In the autumn of 1899, Reinhold Sadler, whose position with the Stewart faction of his party was probably tenuous at best, managed to antagonize the senator and C. C. Wallace in a move that portended ill consequences. Stewart and Wallace attempted to have one of their coterie appointed warden of the Nevada state prison. Sadler refused, asserting that the statutes did not allow him to make the appointment on a political basis. After days of bickering and pressure on the governor, Wallace abandoned the project. He wrote to Stewart then that Sadler was finished politically: "I want you to know that Sadler is a first class son of a bitch. . . . I am asking no favors of him." Wallace indicated that he would bury the governor, given the proper tools.[9]

By November, the state's politicians were fully involved in making plans and working out schemes for the next year's election. Important questions were the problems of leadership and the possibility of fusion of silverite parties in a presidential election year. Sam Davis learned of a plot to oust him as chairman of the Silver party central committee and to reinstall Will Sharon at a proposed meeting in December. Davis wrote to Senator Stewart that he intended to oppose this move as well as another to have both the Democrats and the Silvermen endorse Congressman Newlands for a new term in 1900.[10] Four days later, Davis wrote to Stewart again, saying that plans for a real merger of the two parties would be discussed at the proposed central committee meeting, which would also include the Democratic committee. One proposal in the fusion scheme would permit the Silvermen to name all the candidates on the fall election ticket in return for allowing the Democrats to attach their party's label to the slate. In effect, it would mean the end of the Silver party. Newlands, Davis believed, controlled the leaders but not the rank-and-file Democrats and Silvermen. Davis had advised the Silvermen not to join the "confab," but to wait and see what the Democrats accomplished alone.[11] His ideas gained enough support to postpone the meeting.

Black Wallace also worked against the merger of the two parties in 1900. He believed then that the Silver party might be used "for one campaign more." "Then," he wrote to Stewart, "we must quit." The Wallace-Stewart faction should then organize the Republican party in Nevada, "or be left out in the cold." Under all circumstances, Wallace declared, "we must beat Newlands." Newlands and his supporters, the railroad lobbyist said, were working to fuse the Democrats and Silvermen completely, a project which would spoil his plans for the last campaign.[12]

The Republicans were also fractionated. Not all Democrats or all Silvermen wanted fusion, but they had certain mutual goals and interests. The Republicans, on the other hand, divided not only on the basic silver question, but also on candidates. For example, the Wallace group in the GOP promoted the candidacy of Edward S. Farrington for

Congress in 1900, while the anti-Wallace party wanted to nominate P. L. Flanigan of Reno.[13]

For his part, Francis G. Newlands promoted his ideas for fusion of the "anti-administration" parties locally and nationally.[14] He also furthered his own supremacy in Nevada politics by paying newspapers five to ten dollars a column to print material which he sent them. This practice caused a good deal of protest among opposition groups, but the hard-pressed editors were glad to have the income.[15]

Fusion discussions continued throughout the winter and spring of 1900. Sam Davis represented the men who opposed fusion. He wrote to Senator Stewart that the Silver party should not be abandoned, but that the electoral ticket might be merged "to make things snug and sure for Bryan" in his second attempt to be elected president.[16] Francis Newlands and George Nixon represented those who wished for the fusion, their plans turning mainly on a desire to obtain the Senate seat for Newlands. They must gain control of the fusion forces to elect enough holdover senators in the state legislature and to control other nominations, obviously easier to accomplish with one party than with two. Furthermore, Newlands had lost some of his earlier support in the battle with Stewart in 1898–1899, especially among state officials. It would be difficult to regain this lost faction unless fusion could be managed. The Republicans, fortunately for Newlands, were no stronger than they had been two years before.[17]

Another argument for fusion was advanced by John H. Dennis, chairman of the Democratic state central committee. Dennis wanted to promote his party, which was enjoying a foretaste of state control after years of cooperating with the Silvermen. He proposed that the Democrats invite the Silver party to participate in a joint convention, believing that if the two silverite parties could not join their forces, the Republicans would take the election. Black Wallace was, in February, 1900, working closely with the Republican chiefs and promising them that the Silvermen would join the GOP. Dennis predicted a defeat for a Bryan-led ticket under the circumstances, for a split in the silver forces would give a plurality to the Republicans. Furthermore, with money and free railroad passes—two commodities which he had in plenty—Wallace could ensure a Silver convention which would do his bidding. The Democratic chairman felt that the Democrats should hold their convention and name their candidates and electors before the Silvermen met. Then, if the Silver party nominated opposing candidates, the Wallace scheme would be exposed and the rank-and-file silverites would vote Democratic. Dennis proposed trying to "consolidate the anti-Republican element" in the state, pointing out that Newlands could expect no support from a Wallace-dominated Silver convention, and it would thus be to the congressman's advantage to join in the plan.[18]

By mid-February, Wallace's plan to divide the Silvermen, disconcert the Democrats, and defeat Newlands for Congress with the railroad lawyer Farrington was well in operation. Some observers believed that Farrington would win in a well-organized campaign.[19] Democrats and Silvermen alike realized that they would have to work diligently for their congressional candidate and for the silver cause.[20] The opposition to Newlands was evidently well planned and well financed, at least in the early stages.

Pressing the case for fusion through the late winter, John Dennis wrote for Congressman Newlands's information: "I have it on reliable authority that Sam Davis said [in a proposed fusion] the Democrats could have one elector and no more. My informant was [the] editor of the Reno Weekly Ledger, which has come out as a Democratic paper. He also informed me that Sam assured him there was $250 in it if he would come out in opposition to Newlands. . . ." Several state officials, Dennis continued, were willing to give the Democrats the choice of all electors, but "would under no circumstances stand Newlands." Again, Dennis urged his plan of allowing Wallace to expose his hand in the Silver convention. Meanwhile, the party chairman proposed to enhance Newlands's prestige by naming him to head the delegation at the Democratic national convention, then a few months away.[21] In the interim, the two central committees again planned a joint meeting.

Black Wallace continued to dominate a large segment of the Silver group. He wrote to Senator Stewart: "I hope you will not make yourself conspicuous for Bryan. . . . We will endorse Bryan but will not fuse with the Dems. . . . If Bryan is beaten then the Silver Party gets to the ditch and the old parties will be as they were."[22] A return to the status quo ante Silver would mean that the railroad would again be in firm and quiet control of Nevada government, and the maverick Newlands would be out of politics. Even at that time, Newlands was beginning to show inclinations toward what he later espoused more vigorously: government control and regulation of the nation's transportation systems. Such a man in an important post would certainly be against the railroad's interests.

In the days before the central committees met, Congressman Newlands's prospects for controlling his followers looked bleak indeed, for the fight for reelection was already beset with difficulties. Along with the question of fusion and Black Wallace's activities against him, the financial backers of the Wallace-Stewart brand of politics could not be convinced that Newlands also deserved their support. The Southern Pacific had no intention of restricting Wallace's activities, despite earlier assurances. Collis P. Huntington, president of the corporation, was a dedicated foe of the congressman. Furthermore, if John W. Mackay, the pioneer Nevada miner who was then living in New York and who had supported McKinley in 1896, became a director of the Southern Pacific as planned, Newlands's prospects would be even worse, since Mackay was very influential with some of the state's Democrats. In addition, the John P. Jones group in the Silver party would oppose Newlands because he was a threat to the senator's reelection plans in 1902.[23] A Newlands man in eastern Nevada displayed some understanding of what might be necessary when he wrote to the congressman, "Any 'sacks' to be used in Eureka County this Fall—kindly consider my application. . . ."[24]

The fusion fight, until then mostly in the background, reached the newspapers as the central committees announced their meetings. One proponent of fusion wrote to deplore Black Wallace's intrigues. The railroad man was a "tyrant," he wrote, an evil demoralizing force, the leader of a "gang of enemies to the State." Wallace must be defeated, said the editor of the *Nevada State Journal,* in order to bring decent politics and government to Nevada.[25]

When the Silver state central committee met, Wallace was apparently in control; fusion would be defeated unequivocally. The railroad representative, holding twenty-five proxies, began his battle, confident of complete victory. George Nixon and Will Sharon represented a bloc of twenty-two men. Others on the committee were uncommitted or were assumed by the leaders to be safely in one camp or the other. Wallace's confidence was shaken when an unexpected parliamentary struggle developed. A resolution appointing a "conference committee" to meet with the Democrats passed, and so did a proposal to hold the state convention in the same town at the same time as the Democrats. Even though the Wallace men held—and voted—a proxy apparently issued by a dead man, Reinhold Sadler, Will Sharon, and others were named to a committee to confer with the Democrats on a merger.[26]

Wallace had met with an important defeat for the first time in his long career. Charles M. Sain, Lovelock newspaper editor and a proxy voter in the central committee meeting, wrote in a long letter to Senator Stewart that it was the first time he had ever seen Wallace "in the least disconcerted." Wallace had been more than disconcerted, Sain reported. The ordinarily silken-mannered Wallace had shouted at Sadler, who, he claimed, had been responsible for confusing the issues. Later, when the governor had attempted to explain his actions, the lobbyist had refused to listen, saying that Sadler had "bulled the thing all up [*sic*]."

The Lovelock editor blamed the defeat on underestimating the strength of the opposition:

We lost the fight by talking too much. . . . All we had to do was to pass one resolution . . ., already prepared, and we had the votes to do it. But we went into session at 12 M., and didn't get out until 5, and then lost. . . . We simply talked ourselves to death. . . . We got into the hole by overconfidence. . . . We let Sharon get some of our men. [Then] even after voting down all substitutes the committee unanimously passed a resolution which in effect was the very thing that the opposition had contended for. In my opinion it makes fusion on New-lands almost certain.

The Wallace followers had virtually lost the Silver party, Sain believed. In fact, the Newlands-Sharon leaders had been so skillful that the fall election would be in effect a Democrat-Republican struggle. "I hardly look for a silver party ticket," Sain observed.

The fiasco had also nearly doomed Edward Farrington's chances for the congressional seat, the Lovelock editor continued. Farrington was loyal to the silver cause and could not endorse the gold standard, as some of the Republicans (on whose ticket he now would run) wanted him to do. Furthermore, he was rather a weak candidate for the Wallace people, since he was regarded as "frank and honest," and was expected to refuse to endorse statements that were against his principles. Perhaps worst of all, the Newlands-Sharon political machine had, by the end of April, 1900, captured important newspapers in Virginia City, Carson City, and Reno, establishing a "complete hold" on the press of those areas. In short, to one Stewart supporter at least, the summer and autumn now looked as bleak for the antisilver partisans as the spring had seemed for the fusionists.[27]

The Democratic central committee meeting was as harmonious as the Silver committee's had been disruptive. The Democrats had a good deal to gain from fusion with the popular Silvermen, and if they were skillful, the situation could be made into a great Democratic victory. The Democratic chiefs easily passed the resolution in favor of the merger, and another naming Silvermen Francis G. Newlands, Reinhold Sadler, and C. E. Mack as half the Nevada delegation to the Democratic national convention. The two silverite parties then prepared to meet in Virginia City on September 6, 1900.[28]

The Republicans also met in April to select their delegates to the national convention. At their meeting in Carson City, they endorsed their national leaders and cheered the prosperity they said had resulted from William McKinley's administration. The conclave was described as "harmonious" by a friendly reporter. Allen Bragg of the *Reno Evening Gazette* declared that the Republicans' freedom from the silver issue had made this "the best and ablest" Republican state gathering in eight years.[29]

As the nation prepared for the national political conventions, it became clear that old-style populism was nearly finished. Thomas E. Watson, responding to several requests that he announce his presidential ambitions, told a reporter for the Associated Press that "under no circumstances" would he accept a nomination. He concluded his statement with "Please number me among the politically dead and let me henceforth rest in peace."[30] The silverites would thus adhere again to the Democrat Bryan, who would apparently have a clear field for the presidential nomination. Francis Newlands wrote optimistically before the Democratic national convention that the Nebraskan would "prevent the lawless wealth of the country from controlling it and absolutely changing our form of government."[31]

The Republican national convention met in Philadelphia in June. William McKinley and Theodore Roosevelt received the nominations from a cheering crowd. The GOP chieftains adopted a money plank endorsing the gold standard almost without opposition. In Nevada's financial center at Reno, a salute of "4,000 fire crackers and Chinese bombs" greeted the end of the convention.[32]

The Democrats met during the first week in July, in Kansas City. There, a controversy developed over the financial plank, with some delegates desiring an equivocal statement and others demanding a 16 to 1 declaration. William Jennings Bryan, the certain nominee, declared that he would run only on a platform containing the 16 to 1 pledge. This statement settled an argument that had virtually dominated preconvention maneuvering,[33] although the overriding issue of the following campaign would be condemnation of the imperialism of the Spanish-American war. The Nebraskan was nominated for the presidency almost by acclamation, and Adlai E. Stevenson of Illinois received the second place on the ticket. When Francis G. Newlands returned to Nevada from the convention, he reported that he was pleased at the adoption of the financial plank in the platform and particularly well satisfied with results of his efforts to lead the Democrats to declare themselves in favor of a national system of reclamation of arid western lands.[34]

The Democratic convention spurred some fusion attempts by inviting the leaders of other silverite parties to platform discussions.[35] Only a few national silverite parties attempted to promote independent ideas. The People's party (fusion faction) joined the Democrats in demanding free coinage and condemning imperialism. The People's party (middle-of-the-road faction) argued for all the old Populist reforms, and included a 16 to 1 plank in the platform almost as an afterthought. An abortive attempt to revive the Silver Republican party brought a declaration in favor of bimetallism, and an endorsement of Populist reforms.[36] None of the minor parties gained enough support to obtain even one electoral vote. The era of the silver parties was drawing to an end.

In Nevada, however, the issue of fusion had not yet been settled. It was nevertheless to the obvious advantage of silverite or "anti-imperialist" parties to merge their electoral tickets to assure a united front in the presidential contest. Republicans, on the other hand, still had no real party home if they believed in free silver, for the so-called Silver Republican activities went unnoticed in the state. The problem was reflected in the state Republican party meeting in Virginia City on the last day of August.

The Nevada GOP endorsed William McKinley and the national Republican platform except for the financial plank. The Nevada men asked instead for "the largest use of silver as a money metal compatible with the best interests of our government." The major nomination made by the Republicans was that of E. S. Farrington for Congress. Farrington spoke briefly in acknowledging the honor, taking the occasion to disassociate himself from the Southern Pacific railroad and Black Wallace, denying "emphatically" that he was "in any way connected" with either. After other nominations and routine business, the Republicans adjourned.[37] The Wallace faction had thus controlled the Republican convention; Farrington had been their candidate from the start, of course, despite his brave disclaimer.[38]

Meanwhile, the Silver and Democratic parties prepared for their conventions by placing joint advertisements in the state's newspapers. When the two groups met separately in Virginia City, disagreement was thought to be so deep that no fusion could possibly result. The first session of the Democratic convention was described as "stormy," with frequent recesses and caucuses. Finally, a committee on fusion was appointed to meet with a counterpart from the Silvermen. When the conferees returned to the hall, it was to report that the Silver party had offered the Democrats places on a fused ticket for two presidential electors, a short-term university regent, and the joint nomination of Francis G. Newlands for Congress. The Silver party would select one elector, a long-term regent, and the supreme court justice. The Democrats rejected the proposal, at least partly because they thought that Black Wallace had suggested it. The Democrats also felt that since they were a national party, and it was a presidential election year, they should have the top places on the ticket. The Silvermen, on the other hand, believed that as the majority party they should control the nominations.

A second conference committee was appointed, with the Democrats hoping this time for better treatment. The Silvermen, meanwhile, had accepted the first report, but indicated willingness to reopen the negotiations. The second conference report produced about the same result as the first, except that the group now proposed a joint convention for the nomination of the supreme court justice.

While the Democrats debated the prospect of fusion at Piper's Opera House, the Silvermen convened next door at the Knights of Pythias hall. When the first fusion proposal had been rejected by the Democrats, and the second report was presented, a debate ensued that almost ended in physical violence. Nevertheless, the second report was accepted by the Silvermen, sixty-six votes to twenty-eight. Black Wallace had been outmaneuvered for the second time in a few months by the Newlands men.

The Democratic platform hailed the nominations of William Jennings Bryan and Adlai Stevenson, called for union of the state's "reform forces," endorsed the national party's aims, and held the silver question to be one of the nation's most important problems. The Democrats' platform also congratulated the Silver party on its riddance of William Stewart, who had rejoined the Republicans almost indecently soon after his reelection to the Senate. They suggested that the Southern Pacific railroad devote itself to the development of the state. The Silver party platform was nearly identical to the Democratic statement, with two important differences. The Silver party of Nevada demanded that William Stewart resign as United States senator and recommended that the central committee action ejecting William Sharon and Congressman Newlands from the party in 1899 be expunged from the record.

The two conventions made their separate nominations, as the conference committee had agreed. Newlands was nominated for Congress by acclamation in each hall. After these formalities, the Silvermen joined the Democrats at the Opera House to exchange cheers and messages of good will, and to nominate Adolphus L. Fitzgerald for supreme court justice. Francis Newlands addressed a cheering joint convention.[39]

The Democrats had won and now could see the prospect of gaining control of the state's government after many lean years. The merging of the two parties seemed as solid as possible, and if this fusion could be maintained through the state election in 1902, the Silver party of Nevada would be no more than an important faction of the Democratic party. Francis G. Newlands had also won; he could claim all the privileges of membership in a major party and loyalty to the silver cause at the same time. He had recognized the advantages to be gained in such an association, and adher-

ence to the silver cause by the national Democratic party
had made the path smoother. Thus, through Newlands's
manipulation, and with the proper kind of leadership, the
state might ultimately move into the Democratic column.
Meanwhile, the fall campaign lay ahead, and the state had
to be assured for William Jennings Bryan as well as for
Congressman Newlands.

Prosperity seemed to be returning to Nevada in the summer and early autumn of 1900. Optimism over a possible
revival of mining spread as new discoveries were reported
from Nye, Washoe, and White Pine counties. Livestock
and agriculture offered similar portents. For the first time
in memory, cattlemen in western Nevada sold their beeves
before the end of August, and an important sheepman of
Washoe County reported shipping a huge consignment of
lambs to Chicago. At the same time, real estate dealers in
several Nevada communities told of receiving more inquir-
ies for property than they had had in several years, and
said that prices were higher than they had been for a
decade.[40]

The Southern Pacific and Central Pacific railroads, fully
merged in 1899, were equally prosperous. The value of the
new corporation's stock and earnings in the state increased
by $834,536 over 1899, while taxes paid the state had
accomodatingly been reduced in the same period by slightly
more than $7,000. The company had been able to spend
about a half million dollars for improvements along its
roads since 1899.[41] The rates the railroad charged added to
its profitable operation. Passenger rates of five cents a mile
in Nevada contrasted with two and a half cents in California, while freight rates were chargeable "to tide water"
in California, and backhaul charges at double the fee to

points in Nevada.[42] Railroad charges might have been an issue in the campaign of 1900, and to some extent they were, yet the leading question remained the congressional race between Francis G. Newlands and Edward S. Farrington.

As the contest began, the Republicans were the beneficiaries of some important defections from the Silver ranks. William M. Stewart, declaring that the silver issue was composed only of "political ghosts and hobgoblins,"[43] announced his plan to support the candidacy of William McKinley. Henry R. Mighels, whose Carson City *Morning Appeal* had loyally supported the senator through the campaign of 1898–1899, called Stewart a traitor, a quitter, a deserter under fire. Mighels reminded his readers that "the Silver men of Nevada fought through three campaigns for Stewart," and had "stood in the breech [*sic*] when there was a close prospect that his colors would go down in defeat." Now, said the scribe, the senator's former friends felt "anything but pleasant at the value he placed on their services."[44] At Tuscarora, the disillusioned Silvermen hung Stewart in effigy. The figure, suspended from a flagpole, was decorated with cards saying, "Traitor Stewart," "Borax Bill," "So be it with all traitors," and the like. The dummy dangled in the town's most prominent spot for several days.[45]

Senator Stewart made several speeches during the campaign, for McKinley and for Farrington. However, in their bitterness, or perhaps because their loyalties had been purchased by the opposition, the newspapers of the state refused to print either the speeches or accounts of the rallies where they were delivered.[46] Stewart, for his part, claimed that the silver issue was dead, and complained that the people of Nevada failed to recognize this fact. Furthermore, he felt that his constituents' "unreasonable faith" in Bryanism was unjustified by the realities of the situation. Bryan's speeches on the silver question, Stewart said, went unnoticed outside of Nevada.[47]

As the campaign between Newlands and Farrington began to heighten, the contestants traded charges in traditional fashion. And, in traditional fashion, Newlands declared that he would not reply to personal attacks, but would confine his remarks to issues and principles.[48] Meanwhile, the congressman paid generous sums of money to state newspapers, increased his contributions to church building funds and charity drives, financed an experimental project to pave Reno's Virginia Street, and pressed his party workers to distribute campaign materials in ever increasing volume.[49]

The overall campaign lacked both color and enthusiasm. Various editors tried to make issues of the tariff, of a proposal to legalize lotteries, of the irrigation problem, and so on, but these failed to catch the attention of the voters. A Bryan rally in Reno on September 20, which had been advertised for many days in advance, was almost a complete failure. Newlands and a glee club appeared; three scheduled speakers did not. Finally, the congressman invited the entire audience to join him for a drink at the Riverside Hotel bar; he entertained twenty-five guests and the glee club.[50]

The Republicans fared little better. In Ely, the citizens were surprised by a visit from candidate Farrington. They rather hurriedly arranged a public meeting where Farrington spoke to attack Newlands. The congressman, the challenger claimed, was the tool of C. C. Wallace and allied railroad interests. The candidate also declared that he was in favor of free coinage of silver at 16 to 1, and pledged that if elected, he would work for full remonetization of the white metal.[51] He then distributed a pamphlet entitled "Gold the Best Money Metal—Dangers from the Unlimited Coinage of Silver—How Wage Earners Would Suffer." The ambivalence was not lost on Nevada's electorate.[52]

In the campaign for Bryan, the Silver-Democratic orators on circuit around the state rang the changes on financial reform and remonetization of silver, the abolition or regulation of trusts, and the great moral wrong of imperialism. The speakers for President McKinley talked mainly of the return of prosperity to the West, and of the glory of acquiring an empire for the United States in the Pacific and Caribbean.[53] The Republicans and antisilver people maintained that the silver issue had passed out of existence, and the sooner the Silver party followed, the better.[54]

Although the state races and the congressional contest seemed almost settled from the start, a number of local skirmishes held more excitement. An example of intrigue of some dimensions occurred in White Pine County. There, a situation developed in the election contest for state senator between Silverman H. A. Comins, the incumbent, and Democrat Charles Greene, the challenger. At issue was the winner's vote for United States senator in 1902. Shortly before the election, Congressman Newlands received several telegrams and letters questioning the activities of his supporters in White Pine. Chief among the workers were Sol Hilp and P. C. Weber. Weber was the Democratic political boss of the county and was regarded as very powerful.[55] Hilp was a pioneer merchant of the area's mining camps. Between the two, they controlled the Democratic organization in the eastern county. When the controversy came to light, Will Sharon wired his relative: "Received the following telegram . . . Hilp has bushels of money for Greene where did he get it signed Decker. My answer all I can say know nothing about Hilp always supposed he was against us."[56] E. H. Decker, editor of the *White Pine News,* wired Newlands himself: "Hilp is hurting your fight by strong work for Greene. Call him off if possible."[57] A few days later, Decker wrote to Newlands, telling him that Hilp and Weber had had a "sack" of at least $1,500, which they had used to elect Greene. He resented the defeat of Comins, a loyal Silverman, by the Democrat Greene,[58] and was apparently innocent of a secret agreement reached between Newlands and the new state senator elect.

The explanation of what happened in White Pine County in 1900 came in a letter from P. C. Weber to Newlands following the election. Weber congratulated the congressman on his reelection and remarked that he and Hilp had had a difficult but rewarding battle in electing Greene, who had promised to support Newlands's aspiration for the Senate seat in 1902.[59] Presumably, despite his earlier loyalties, no such commitment was forthcoming from Comins. Sol Hilp moved his family to Reno and entered business there, awaiting a federal appointment. Like many other political expectations, this was fated for disappointment, for the supposed assurances came to nothing.[60]

The expense of the campaign, while burdensome, was not more than the wealthy Newlands could bear. Moreover, he and Will Sharon won several thousands of dollars by betting on Newlands to win the congressional seat.[61] For their part, the Republicans were reported to have spent $50,000 to promote their candidates in 1900.[62] They might as well have saved their money. The Silver-Democrat electors polled more than 60 percent of the vote; Newlands won by a majority of 1,785 over Farrington, and Judge Fitzgerald led the ticket.[63] Summarizing the results of the national election, the editor of the *Appeal* wrote: "Nevada is true blue and her vote goes where it has for the past eight years for a losing candidate, but one whom the people trust. Nevada has not endorsed the gold bug policy of the Administration."[64] William McKinley had won the presidency easily, and by a margin larger than four years before.

William Stewart digested the election results in a letter to a friend, J. R. DeLamar, a few days later. He was persuaded that both Bryanism and the Silver party were dead at last. After informing his friend that John P. Jones would retire in 1902, Stewart wrote: "Mr. Newlands is elected to Congress after the expenditure of vast sums of money. . . . He had made his bed in the Democratic party, which . . . will again be the minority party. . . . If you would like to go to the Senate from Nevada the way is clear, and with proper effort the result is certain. . . . If you desire the place and are willing to spend some money . . . I will assist you."[65]

A month later, Stewart wrote again, assuring DeLamar that Newlands was so weakened by the late campaign fight that any good Republican would be able to defeat him for the Senate seat in 1902.[66] The senator continued to search for candidates to oppose Newlands, without much success, for the next two years. The senator was old, out of favor with Silvermen and Democrats, and not greatly admired by the members of his own party. Nevertheless, he exercised his prerogatives of dispensing patronage and attempting to maintain at least the vestiges of his former political power, always with the goal of defeating or discrediting Congressman Newlands. That possibility was still in the future, however, for Newlands was safely ensconced in Congress for another two years and had already announced that he would, indeed, be a candidate for the Senate in 1902.

NOTES

[1] Nevada, State Legislature, *Appendix to the Journals of the Senate and Assembly,* Nineteenth Session (1899). Governor Sadler's message.

[2] *Nevada State Journal,* February 2, 1899, p. 3; *Statutes of Nevada,* Nineteenth Session (1899), Ch. cvii, p. 128.

[3] *Statutes of Nevada,* Nineteenth Session, Ch. lxxi, pp. 86–87.

[4] *Morning Appeal,* March 13, 1899, p. 2.

[5] *Nevada State Journal,* March 22, 1899, p. 2.

[6] George Nixon to Francis G. Newlands, March 28, 1899. Newlands papers.

[7] William Stewart to Mrs. Nellie Bonnifield, Carson City, April 21, 1899; Stewart to Collis P. Huntington, April 21, 1899. Stewart papers.

[8] William Stewart to Gordon Clark, Boston, Massachusetts, May 20, 1899. Stewart papers.

[9] C. C. Wallace to William Stewart, October 26, 1899. Stewart papers.

[10] Sam Davis to William Stewart, November 24, 1899. Stewart papers.

[11] Sam Davis to William Stewart, November 28, 1899. Stewart papers.

[12] C. C. Wallace to William Stewart, December 2, 1899. Stewart papers.

[13] Clarence D. Van Duzer to Francis G. Newlands, January 5, 1900. Newlands papers.

[14] Francis G. Newlands to John H. Dennis, January 11, 1900. Newlands papers.

[15] Francis G. Newlands to William Sharon, January 2, 1900. Newlands papers. The practice of purchasing favorable publicity

was fairly effective; even Black Wallace recognized its impact and tried to promote a similar project for Stewart, but without notable success.

[16] Sam Davis to William Stewart, January 27, 1900. Stewart papers.

[17] George Nixon to Francis G. Newlands, February 8, 1900. Newlands papers.

[18] John Hancock Dennis to Joseph R. Ryan, February 2, 1900. Newlands papers. The letter was obviously intended for Newlands's consideration, and was duly forwarded to him by Will Sharon.

[19] Marion S. Wilson, Elko, Nevada, to Francis G. Newlands, February 16, 1900. Newlands papers.

[20] Joseph Ryan to William Sharon, February 20, 1900. Newlands papers.

[21] John H. Dennis to Joseph Ryan, March 5, 1900. Newlands papers.

[22] C. C. Wallace to William Stewart, March 10, 1900. Stewart papers.

[23] William Sharon to Francis G. Newlands [April, 1900]. Newlands papers. The reference to John W. Mackay's support of President McKinley is in a letter, William M. Stewart to John W. Mackay, April 2, 1897. Stewart papers.

[24] B. L. Smith, Eureka, Nevada, to Francis G. Newlands, March 28, 1900. Newlands papers.

[25] *Nevada State Journal,* April 10, 1900.

[26] *Ibid.,* April 13, 1900, p. 3.

[27] Charles M. Sain to William Stewart, April 21, 1900. Stewart papers.

[28] *Nevada State Journal,* April 15, 1900, p. 3.

[29] *Reno Evening Gazette,* April 20, 1900, p. 3; April 21, 1900, p. 2.

[30] *Ibid.,* April 27, 1900, p. 1.

[31] Francis G. Newlands to James Merriam, New York, May 26, 1900. Newlands papers.

[32] *Reno Evening Gazette,* June 21, 1900, p. 3.

[33] *New York Times,* July 3, 1900, pp. 1–2.

[34] *Nevada State Journal,* July 17, 1900, p. 3.

[35] *New York Times,* July 4, 1900, p. 2.

[36] Kirk H. Porter and Donald B. Johnson, comps., *National Party Platforms, 1840–1956* (Urbana: University of Illinois Press, 1956), pp. 112–126. See also, *New York Times,* July 5, 1900, p. 2.

[37] *Territorial Enterprise,* August 31, 1900, p. 1; *Reno Evening Gazette,* August 31, 1900, p. 1.

[38] C. C. Wallace to William Stewart, March 10, 1900: "I have sprung Farrington as [the railroad] candidate he can beat Newlands." Stewart papers.

[39] *Territorial Enterprise,* September 7, 1900, p. 1; *Morning Appeal,* September 7, 1900, p. 3.

[40] Reports of prosperity were general throughout the state. See especially: *Nevada State Journal,* July 28, 1900, p. 1, on prospects in the Robinson (White Pine County) District; July 31, 1900, p. 3, on Washoe County mining business; *Reno Evening Gazette,* August 24, 1900, p. 3, and August 29, 1900, p. 3, on agriculture and real estate transactions. See also: Russell R. Elliott, *Nevada's Twentieth-Century Mining Boom* (Reno: University of Nevada Press, 1966).

[41] *Reno Evening Gazette,* August 9, 1900, p. 2.

[42] *Ibid.,* August 13, 1900, p. 2.

[43] *Morning Appeal,* August 27, 1900, p. 2.

[44] *Ibid.,* August 22, 1900, p. 3.

[45] *Ibid.,* August 29, 1900, p. 3.

[46] Charles J. Kappler to George T. Mills, October 24, 1900. Stewart papers.

[47] William M. Stewart, *Reminiscences* . . . (New York, 1908), p. 318.

[48] Francis G. Newlands to A. C. May, Elko, Nevada, September 14, 1900. Newlands papers.

[49] See many letters in Newlands papers, August to November, 1900. An account of the Reno street-paving experiment appeared in the *Reno Evening Gazette,* August 25, 1900, p. 3, and August 31, 1900, p. 1.

[50] *Reno Evening Gazette,* September 21, 1900, p. 3.

[51] *Ibid.,* September 22, 1900, p. 3.

[52] *Morning Appeal,* October 24, 1900, p. 3.

[53] See especially: *Reno Evening Gazette,* July 24, 1900, p. 3; *Morning Appeal,* October 27, 1900, p. 3.

[54] *Reno Evening Gazette,* October 20, 1900, p. 3.

[55] Charles D. Gallagher, "Memoir and Autobiography," typescript of an oral history interview, conducted by Mary Ellen Glass for the Oral History Project of the Center for Western North American Studies, University of Nevada, 1965, p. 35. P. C. Weber was generally referred to as "Boss" Weber.

[56] Telegram, William Sharon to Francis G. Newlands, November 4, 1900. Newlands papers.

[57] Telegram, E. H. Decker to Francis G. Newlands, November 4, 1900. Newlands papers.

[58] E. H. Decker to Francis G. Newlands, November 8, 1900. Newlands papers.

[59] P. C. Weber to Francis G. Newlands, November 9, 1900. Newlands papers.

[60] Lester J. Hilp, "Reminiscences of a White Pine County Native, Reno Pharmacy Owner, and Civic Leader," typescript of an oral history interview, conducted by Mary Ellen Glass for the Oral History Project of the Center for Western North American Studies, University of Nevada, 1967, p. 6.

[61] Telegrams, William Sharon to Francis G. Newlands, November 6, 1900, and November 7, 1900. Newlands papers.

[62] *Morning Appeal*, November 9, 1900, p. 3.

[63] Nevada, Secretary of State, *Political History of Nevada, 1965*, p. 187.

[64] *Morning Appeal*, November 7, 1900, p. 3.

[65] William Stewart to J. R. DeLamar, November 17, 1900. Stewart papers.

[66] William Stewart to J. R. DeLamar, December 18, 1900. Stewart papers.

VIII

The End of Silver Party
Independence

As the twentieth session of the Nevada state legislature prepared to meet in January, 1901, a Reno observer remarked a new peculiarity in Nevada politics: "Among the chief absentees from the . . . Legislature is . . . 'Black Charley,' who has evidently come to the conclusion that it is safe to trust the business of organizing to the members and that 'my people' [the Southern Pacific] will not suffer by his absence. I do not know . . . the reason for the absence of the 'black man,' who has been the motive power of nearly all Nevada legislatures . . . for upwards of twenty years."[1]

Wallace's defeat in the election campaigns of 1900 had apparently caused his removal from the state, and a new era opened. The lobbyist told a friend that he was "absolutely out of Nevada politics," and planned never to take an interest again.[2] When it became apparent that Francis G. Newlands's protégé, Clarence D. Van Duzer, would be elected speaker of the state assembly, Allen Bragg of the *Reno Evening Gazette* wrote that the event was Wallace's "death knell."[3] He unwittingly wrote the truth; the most powerful manipulator of Nevada's politics to that time died on January 31, in California, where he had gone to inspect some mining property.

No longer would the meetings of all public and semi-public bodies be subject to this master politician. Gone now was the talent that had given his adopted state a coherent political and governmental system that served "my people." Wallace's favorite method of establishing his political view had been to "combine the elements," provided, of course, that the elements were combined as he wished. Although the lobbyist was often regarded as a bad adviser in his role as legislative advocate for the Central Pacific and Southern Pacific, even his severest critics admitted that some of the laws enacted under his supervision were good. For twenty years, at least, the man had worked to "line up the people" in the interest of the railroad and, it seems reasonable to assume, in the interest of his own political power.[4] At any rate, the lawmakers of 1901 wasted little time in mourning their dead taskmaster and turned to the business of the session.

A Republican editor wrote that he would forgive the Silver-Democrats for past "sins" if the legislature defeated the proposal for a state lottery, repealed the prizefight law, and reformed the state's tax structure.[5] One suggestion for financial reform was that the state enter the reclamation business, construct dams, and sell the water.[6] The lottery idea, however, dominated the discussions at the beginning.

In 1899, the legislature had approved an amendment to the state constitution which would allow the holding of lotteries in the state. A second favorable vote from the 1901 legislature would leave only a ballot by the voters to effect the change. Powerful, nonpartisan opposition developed. One petition published by nearly two dozen judges, lawyers, and politicians demanded defeat for the scheme.[7] All three major political parties in Nevada had repudiated the plan, and many legislators had run for office on an antilottery platform.[8]

The issue also dominated the organization of the legislature. The forces in favor of the lottery scheme attempted to control the election of the speaker of the assembly. When this proved unsuccessful, they tried to control the selection of committees and were again voted down. The organization of the legislature continued then with the antilottery (Newlands) faction in control.[9]

Governor Sadler ignored the lottery problem when he addressed the lawmakers. In spite of the evident economic growth, Sadler was still pessimistic. He blamed the continued hard times on "unfriendly legislation" by the United States Congress, which discriminated against silver as a money metal. Nevertheless, Sadler said the state was in sound financial condition; the debt was down to $242,000, and taxes were sufficient to meet appropriations unless expenditures increased materially. He again begged the legislators not to "overlook anything that promises relief" from the state's financial woes. He recommended leaving reclamation and water storage problems to the national authorities, but suggested that the lawmakers might enact measures to prevent wastage of water. No major requests followed; the governor said that he had been ill and was

unable to work out a full program.[10] The men were thus
left to their own devices, without advice from the governor
on their most pressing problem. It was generally believed,
however, that Sadler would sign a lottery amendment if
the legislature passed it.[11]

The lobby in favor of the lottery amendment was extremely active, with a state senator from Ormsby County
reportedly carrying a "sack" for the lottery corporation.
Other prolottery leaders included Lieutenant Governor
James R. Judge and several senators and assemblymen.[12]
Some of the latter had been in the group that was corrupted
in the 1899 Senate election, but in 1901 there was no effective or organized leadership to cement their alliances. The
railroad had apparently decided to take no active part in
the contest.[13]

Francis G. Newlands was an important leader against the
proposal. He conducted a good deal of research among his
congressional colleagues and then declared that he was
unequivocally opposed to a state lottery.[14] The *Reno Evening Gazette*'s editor, unaccustomed to praising the congressman, called this position "a manly stand."[15] Newlands
continued to oppose the amendment and offered a donation
of a hundred dollars for an educational campaign.[16] He also
asserted that if the state passed a lottery law, the immoral
connotations would make it difficult for him, as a representative of the state, to press his irrigation proposals.[17]

The much discussed amendment was presented in the
legislature as Senate Concurrent Resolution 11. A motion
to kill the proposal received only three negative votes in
the lower house. A similar resolution passed the senate with
only three dissents. The quick action was regarded as a
parliamentary coup by the antilottery forces. The promoters

of the gambling proposal were caught off guard and were described as disconcerted at their lack of foresight.[18] The backers of the lottery could hardly believe that they had failed, even when confronted with the *Gazette*'s two-inch headlines, "Lottery Defeated." Although the men continued to try for passage and planned to import a professional lobbyist from California,[19] the proposition was defeated at its final trial.[20]

The affair had been handled so smoothly that George Nixon could write that the scheme had never had a real chance of being enacted into law. "The truth is," he said, "there was much more talk about the matter than there was any reason for, because at no time was there any strength behind the scheme—no money, no brains, nor anything else that is formible [*sic*] in such contests."[21] Nevertheless, the lottery proposal had given the press something to write about, and had allowed Francis Newlands to put himself publicly on the side of "morality."

When the twentieth session of the Nevada state legislature adjourned, notably absent from the list of resolutions and memorials was the usual demand for free and unlimited coinage of silver. No such resolution was introduced in either house. The lawmakers did, however, pass two separate memorials calling for direct popular election of United States senators. Again, perhaps in reflection of a small number of new laws, the Nevada and United States constitutions, with an index to each, were printed in the *Statutes*.[22]

Summarizing the work of nearly two months, the *Reno Evening Gazette* editor said that the twentieth session had done little good, but as long as the legislators had "done nothing to bring discredit on Nevada," the scribe refused to criticize.[23] The *Morning Appeal*'s editor congratulated the lawmakers on having a meeting free of scandal, and on the fact that "no breath of corruption" had marred the conclave.[24] If the *Appeal*'s word could be trusted, it was the first time in many years that the lawmakers had resisted the blandishments of special interests.

One important act passed by the legislature was little noted or debated during the session, although it received a great deal of local comment following the meeting. Entitled "An Act to provide for a more uniform valuation and assessment of property in this State," the new law provided that county assessors, meeting together as a board, should "establish throughout the State a uniform valuation of all classes of property which, by their character, will admit of such uniform valuation."[25] The first action of the Board of County Assessors under the so-called revenue act was to increase valuations of the Central Pacific railroad properties by $5 million. Spokesmen for the corporation promised a stiff fight to have the raises declared illegal in federal court.[26]

The Central Pacific's suit against the fourteen county assessors began with a request for an injunction in the District Court of the United States in Carson City, where Judge Thomas P. Hawley presided. The railroad attorneys argued on constitutional and statutory grounds that the Board of County Assessors had acted wrongly in nearly doubling the assessment. Attorney General William Woodburn, assisted by several other attorneys, defended the county assessors. Judge Hawley's opinion, very long and somewhat labored, declared that the county assessors had exceeded their authority in valuing only the Central Pacific's property as a class. Had they valued *all* railroad property without naming the Central Pacific, Hawley implied, the injunction would have been denied. In view of the circumstances, however, the judge felt compelled to grant the railroad corporation's request.[27]

Judge Hawley's decision left the Board of County Assessors in confusion. His failure to rule on the constitutionality of the statute left them no choice but to assess property on the old basis until the next statutory meeting of the board in January, 1902. Nevertheless, the corporation, probably realizing that the old order of Black Wallace was gone forever, agreed after a meeting to a higher assessment. By this action, $2 million (instead of $5 million) was added to the state's tax rolls.[28] Finally, District Judge S. J. Bonnifield of Winnemucca declared the Revenue Act of 1901 unconstitutional in a Humboldt County case,[29] and the assessors were relieved of their dilemma. Judge Hawley had avoided alienating the state's officials too severely and had certainly incurred the favor of the railroad.

Nevada's relationships with the railroad improved markedly during 1901. The legislature appointed a committee to establish lines of communication between the corporation and the state's politicians, and following a conference between the delegation and Charles M. Hays, the president of the railroad, hopes for better treatment quickened. The legislative committee believed that the state might soon have lower rates and fares for transportation.[30] Furthermore, editors and speakers who had customarily damned the corporation began to soften their attitudes and to declare that the new climate would bring about better practices on both sides.[31] The demise of Black Wallace had indeed contributed to a change of atmosphere.

Other hopes for improvement in the state's economic condition found a basis in the mining boom in southern

Nevada. And, in the Congress, Francis Newlands pursued prosperity for his state through legislation providing for reclamation of arid lands. Throughout 1901 and extending into 1902, the congressman wrote and spoke constantly of his hopes for a proposed law. He drafted a bill providing that the receipts from sales of public lands be applied to reclamation and, seeking support in the Senate, exchanged letters and notes with Senator Henry C. Hansbrough of North Dakota, who then cosponsored the proposal.[32]

Had their relationships not been so strained, Newlands and Senator Stewart might have cooperated in working out the reclamation act, but Stewart would have none of this. The Nevada senator criticized and belittled the congressman constantly, writing to friends that the bill had little chance of passage, for it was "impossible to pass any general irrigation bill."[33] Stewart wrote also that Newlands's sponsorship of the plan had actually "injured" the cause of reclamation, and that he, himself, would have nothing to do with the bill.[34]

When the Newlands Reclamation Act passed in June, 1902, the congressman was elated. In spite of powerful opposition, he and Senator Hansbrough had steered to enactment the first major progressive measure.[35] In an ill-tempered note to the *Carson News,* William Stewart tried to claim that Theodore Roosevelt, not Newlands, had been responsible for the Reclamation Act.[36]

Meanwhile, although he devoted a great deal of energy to advancing the reclamation cause, Congressman Newlands was compelled to work in Nevada's local politics. He labored constantly to maintain the fusion of silverite forces that he had engineered in 1900, since the ballots had hardly been counted in that election before he announced he would be a candidate for United States senator in 1902. He continued to subsidize friendly newspapers, furthering the cause by acquiring an interest in the *Nevada State Journal.* The editor, John H. Dennis, then distributed political material to other state papers.[37] By early 1902, this activity had resulted in the creation by Newlands of a financial dependency, not only of the *Journal,* but also of several other publications in all sections of the state.[38] This was meant to prepare the way for a Silver-Democratic fusion and victory in the 1902 elections. To this end, Newlands and his supporters devoted their attention from the summer of 1901 until the 1902 election.

As early as July, 1901, the *Nevada State Journal* began to carry articles favoring Newlands's candidacy. In one piece, editor Dennis wrote that the senator who would be elected in 1902 "must be the antipodes of the last United States Senator elected from this state." The scribe listed, among other attributes, that the new senator would need to be well informed on irrigation and reclamation, and a "staunch bimetallist."[39] Dennis wrote a few days later that William Stewart, now far from the bimetallist side, was advocating the candidacy of Marcus Alonzo Hanna, an arch gold bug, for president of the United States.[40]

John P. Jones also received some pointed remarks from the *Journal* editor. The senior senator spent some ten hours in the state in October, 1901, and Dennis commented, "It was rather a prolonged visit for him." The senator told a reporter that he had returned to the Republican party, and that he would support a GOP man for senator "with all my heart." The silver issue, Jones had decided, was "dead."[41] Stewart agreed with his colleague and reported that the Silver party of Nevada was merely a joke in the East; he promised to stump the state for the Republican ticket in 1902. The Democratic editor opined that Stewart would help the Democrats by campaigning for the GOP more than would "a score of the best friendly speakers."[42]

Francis Newlands and William Sharon meanwhile plotted to preserve the fusion they had attained by exerting pressure on state officials and party leaders. Sharon thought that defections from party councils had hurt chances for making the merger permanent. He wrote, "I find all of the state officers from the Governor down are very much disturbed over the desertions from the Silver Party." The apostate faction, Sharon feared, might obstruct the plans for final fusion. A second difficulty, he believed, was that the Republicans were gaining in the ability to gather a rather large "sack," and would ultimately be able to outbid the Silvermen for state senators. It was necessary to prevent this, if possible, for holdover senators might be persuaded to reelect William Stewart in 1904—a calamity to be avoided.[43] Therefore, fusion became increasingly important in the discussions between Sharon, Newlands, and their supporters; the Newlands-subsidized press began early in the year to promote the idea, calling the Silver-Democrats the "fusion party," ignoring the full label.[44] The men all did their work well. When the state central committees of the two parties met in March, 1902, the chiefs agreed that refusal to merge would mean "the surrender of the State government and our representation in the national legislature to the common enemy." As far as the party leaders were concerned, then, fusion would be merely a formality when the state conventions met in August. It was still uncertain whether there would be two conventions or one.[45]

Following the central committee meetings, the Silver and

Democratic party chieftains published a joint "address" to the voters of the state. The statement scored the Republicans for abandoning bimetallism and accused Senators Jones and Stewart of treason to the silver cause and of subservience to the special interests. The leaders declared their pride in the accomplishments of state officials and Francis G. Newlands over the decade and, on the basis of this record, asked for support from the voters for a proposed "Fusion" ticket in the fall elections.[46]

The next step was to assure fusion of the parties at the grass-roots level. Newlands advised his workers to organize Fusion clubs in the various counties and to avoid supporting or opposing individual candidates until this work was completed.[47] The fusion of all forces would help to ensure the congressman's title to the Senate seat, although few people believed that he would have real difficulty. Even many leading Republicans had decided that Newlands had earned a promotion.[48] Other hopeful candidates were not so fortunate. A major worry among supporters of fusion was the possibility of disagreement over places on the election ballot, so most arguments about the worth of the merger turned on endorsement of candidates.[49]

For their part, the Republicans were somewhat disarrayed. Rumors circulated that the GOP had allowed its state organization to fall apart. While party leaders denied that this was so, they admitted that they would have a very tough fight in the fall. The Southern Pacific had nearly decided to refuse support to the Republicans, or at least not to oppose Francis Newlands in his race for the Senate. The consequence of this was that leading Republicans had discussed the possibility of engaging in an antirailroad campaign. George T. Mills, the Republican state chairman and nephew of railroad magnate D. O. Mills, wrote to Senator Stewart that he regarded the decision of the railroad as "incomprehensible." A Democratic senator and state legislature could only harm the railroad's interests. The real wrongs committed by the corporation, Mills felt, could easily become rallying points for opposition forces in the campaign, and it would "require some diplomacy to prevent them from becoming the issues" in the contest. The Republican chairman warned that the railroad would regret its course if it forced the GOP to take a new stance.[50] The Republicans were only beginning to realize their problems in the summer of 1902; the railroad was about to attempt a coup of its own.

Late in July, 1902, Thomas P. Hawley announced that he would be a candidate for the United States Senate in the fall elections. Hawley was then seventy-two years old, robust, and widely respected. Born in 1830 in Indiana, the candidate had gone to California while still young. He practiced law in Nevada City, California, for some fifteen years and, from 1863 to 1865, was district attorney of Nevada County. In 1868, he moved to White Pine County, Nevada, where he followed his profession until 1872. He was elected to the Nevada Supreme Court in 1872 and reelected in 1878. He moved from the supreme bench to the United States Circuit Court, Nevada district; by 1902, he had been nearly twenty years in the federal court.[51] He was about to collect his due from the decision he had rendered in the county assessors' case.

Immediately, William Stewart began to work in the judge's behalf. He visited with the railroad representatives in New York and reported that they were pleased with the candidate. He reminded William F. Herrin, the railroad's legal representative, that a Newlands victory would make the corporation "a great deal of trouble." On the other hand, "The election of Hawley would bury the opposition and secure exemption from annoyance for many years to come."[52] A party leader in Nevada wrote to the senator that Hawley's announcement "fell like a thunderbolt" in the north central part of the state. Most people had felt that Newlands would have no opposition at all, but the prospect of a contest had now revitalized the GOP.[53]

When Stewart wrote to congratulate Hawley on his candidacy, he promised help from D. O. Mills and said that he expected Newlands's finances would be less than the judge's. The senator offered his own assistance to the candidate and discussed using as campaign material some supposed statements by Theodore Roosevelt that he and Newlands had never discussed reclamation, despite the congressman's claim to the contrary.[54] In August, the senator visited Nevada and spent a good deal of time in proclaiming his support of Hawley's plans. He also entertained Republican party chiefs and Southern Pacific railroad officials on a boat trip on Lake Tahoe.

When the senator left the state rather suddenly following the lake cruise, opposition critics speculated that the Republicans has asked him to leave; his unpopularity was so great that his support of Hawley might cause the judge's defeat. Other reasons advanced for Stewart's somewhat precipitous departure included an idea that he had gone east to raise more money for Hawley's campaign.[55]

The Republican leaders could hardly have expressed publicly any emotion except joy at Thomas Hawley's candidacy, but other people were less friendly. Rank-and-file Republicans showed little enthusiasm. Opposition critics made statements ranging from sarcastic to venomous. Some called the candidacy "incomprehensible" or "peculiar," while others asserted that election was "scarcely within the range of political possibility."[56] The Newlands press declared, "With Stewart for his sponsor, no candidate for United States Senator could be elected in Nevada even if his party was in the majority."[57] The *Reno Evening Gazette*'s Allen Bragg loyally supported the Republican and called him "the strongest man that could have been named."[58] Fusion of the silverite forces now became more important than before, for a revitalized GOP was likely to be difficult to subdue.

The issue was not settled when the conventions met in Reno at the end of August, 1902. Furthermore, several candidates had declared their intentions of running for various offices—most notably, Reinhold Sadler for governor. Another candidate for governor had made no public announcement, but had been corresponding with Francis G. Newlands through Senator Fred T. Dubois of Idaho for about a month concerning his chances for the office. The "dark horse" was John Sparks of Washoe County. Newlands had not shown marked enthusiasm for the Sparks candidacy, noting "complications" which might prevent election.[59] The major complication was that Sparks was a gold-standard man and had announced his intention to vote for William McKinley in 1900.[60] Throughout the early spring, Newlands and Will Sharon had regarded Sadler as the strongest candidate for governor on a fusion ticket.[61]

John Sparks was nevertheless exceedingly popular in both the eastern and western sections of the state. He had come to northeastern Nevada from Texas and with his partner, John Tinnin, had built a cattle empire. He later moved to

Washoe County, where he had a ranch near Reno. Sparks was one of the first ranchers to raise blooded stock in the state; his Herefords took a first prize at the World's Columbian Exposition in Chicago in 1893. Tall, handsome, wealthy, and exuding the atmosphere of the frontier, Sparks had hundreds of friends all over the state.[62] Reinhold Sadler, on the other hand, after nearly two full terms as governor, had made his share of enemies and mistakes.

Sadler had been working for several weeks in his own behalf and was expected to make a strong fight. He supposedly had a majority of the Silver convention delegates pledged to his candidacy as the group convened.[63] However, despite an abortive early attempt to force Sadler's nomination, the governor was convinced by the merger advocates to step aside to preserve unity. In his remarks upon assuming the chairmanship of the convention, Sadler expressed his hope that fusion would be achieved. In this hope, he continued, he was willing to sacrifice his own ambitions.[64]

The fusionists in the Democratic and Silver parties continued to work. The two conventions received identical invitations to visit the Newlands home, and following their acceptance, fusion was assured. The Democrats made the major nominations: John Sparks for governor, Clarence D. Van Duzer for Congress. The Silvermen nominated Lem Allen of Churchill County for lieutenant governor. Other nominations were about equally divided. Both platforms demanded free coinage of silver. Francis G. Newlands's desire to be a United States senator received the unanimous endorsement of the joint convention that followed.[65]

Newlands's address to the joint convention seemed quite unlike the hundreds of speeches that had brought the silver movement—and Francis G. Newlands—into prominence. Now the senatorial candidate demanded only "reform," not of the financial structure of the nation, but reform in the larger sense. The fusionists could become a party which would "see that labor receives its proper reward, . . . that the few do not spoliate the many, . . . that the profits of production are properly distributed among all of God's creatures, and that monopoly shall die."[66]

The Republicans met in Reno two weeks later. They realized that all of their enemies had united against them, so they tried to present a harmonious aspect. The top places on the GOP ticket went to A. C. Cleveland for governor and E. S. Farrington for Congress, with Judge Hawley receiving the endorsement for senator. George T. Mills introduced a resolution that claimed full credit for the Reclamation Act for President Theodore Roosevelt. The platform contained an equivocal plank on the money question which used the word "silver" three times in the same sentence.[67]

An important fall campaign lay ahead, but party issues now were secondary to personalities. Clearly, no matter which party won the election, the Silver party of Nevada was finished: the Silver-Democratic candidate for governor was a gold-standard man and the GOP gave lip service to silver only when it was useful. Perhaps because of this situation, the canvass had little of the color and spirit of the past decade, except for the highlight of a tour of the state by William Jennings Bryan. In a speech in Reno, Bryan made the expected remarks about the silver question and denied that the cause was dead. He claimed that the nation's economy was unsound, despite evident prosperity. In his partisan comments, the former presidential aspirant asserted that only the Democrats could redress the grievances of labor against capital. One observer noted that while Bryan endorsed the "Fusion" ticket, he failed to praise one major candidate—John Sparks. Allen Bragg, editor of the Republican *Reno Evening Gazette,* decided that Bryan oratory and themes were out of fashion and pointed out that Theodore Roosevelt, a Republican president, led the nation in improving labor conditions.[68]

During the campaign, a controversy arose when Newlands's supporters failed to have his name certified for the ballot; only Thomas Hawley would appear as a senatorial candidate on the election sheets, under the new regulations adopted in 1899. The legislature had intended to allow a popular choice of candidates by providing for the listing of their names on the ballot, with the legislators morally bound to select the man with the highest tally. Republicans were forced, under the circumstances, to advertise that it was necessary not only to vote for Judge Hawley, but also to vote for GOP members of the legislature. Offered an opportunity to have his name on the ballot, even though it was legally too late for the printing, Newlands refused. He gave as his excuse that the voters might not understand that they must also vote for the correct legislative ticket to assure his election.[69] The senatorial hopeful thereupon made campaign contributions to friendly legislative candidates, reportedly in amounts from $250 to $500.[70] Direct election of senators thus failed its first test in Nevada.

When the canvass was finished, the Silver-Democrats had lost only three contests, all by less than 275 votes. Only one major office, that of secretary of state, went to the Republicans.[71] George T. Mills wrote that the 1902 election was a "severe blow," a "wreck" for the GOP.[72] In the major races, John Sparks became the governor, and Francis G. Newlands, having carried his legislative ticket, would become the United States senator succeeding John P. Jones.

The election ended the independent life of the Silver party. In previous state elections, the Silvermen had refused to merge with other silverites, preferring to nominate and elect their own men. However, fusion in national election years had proved that strength lay in joining with a major party with a national base. The Democrats' adoption of the free-silver cause in 1896, and again in 1900, had given the Silvermen hope of national support. Moreover, the Silver politicians could not ignore the fact that the Democratic party offered patronage and preferment they could not expect to attain for themselves.

NOTES

[1] *Reno Evening Gazette,* January 21, 1901, p. 1.

[2] *Morning Appeal,* February 2, 1901, p. 3.

[3] *Reno Evening Gazette,* January 25, 1901, p. 1.

[4] *San Francisco Chronicle,* January 31, 1901, p. 7; *Nevada State Journal,* January 31, 1901, p. 3; *Reno Evening Gazette,* January 31, 1901, p. 3.

[5] *Reno Evening Gazette,* January 8, 1901, p. 2.

[6] *Ibid.,* January 19, 1901, p. 2.

[7] *Ibid.,* January 4, 1901, p. 3.

[8] *Ibid.,* January 9, 1901, p. 2; January 12, 1901, p. 1.

[9] Clarence D. Van Duzer to Francis G. Newlands, January 29, 1901. Newlands papers.

[10] Nevada, State Legislature, *Appendix to the Journals of the Senate and Assembly,* Twentieth Session (1901). Governor Sadler's message.

[11] *Reno Evening Gazette,* January 19, 1901, p. 3.

[12] *Ibid.,* January 22, 1901, pp. 1 and 3; January 23, 1901, p. 1.

[13] *Reno Evening Gazette,* January 24, 1901, p. 1; *Morning Appeal,* January 15, 1901, p. 3.

[14] Francis G. Newlands to *Nevada State Journal,* January 18, 1901. Newlands papers.

[15] *Reno Evening Gazette,* January 18, 1901, p. 3.

[16] Francis G. Newlands to Joseph E. Stubbs, December 20, 1900. Newlands papers. Stubbs was the president of the state university.

[17] *Morning Appeal,* January 27, 1901, p. 2.

[18] *Reno Evening Gazette,* January 22, 1901, p. 1; January 23, 1901, p. 1.

[19] *Ibid.,* January 24, 1901, p. 2; January 22, 1901, p. 1.

[20] Nevada, State Legislature, *Journal of the Senate,* Twentieth Session (1901), pp. 56–57.

[21] George Nixon to Francis G. Newlands, February 6, 1901. Newlands papers.

[22] *Statutes of Nevada,* Twentieth Session (1901). See also *Journals* of the senate and assembly, 1901.

[23] *Reno Evening Gazette,* March 11, 1901, p. 2.

[24] *Morning Appeal,* March 14, 1901, pp. 2 and 3.

[25] *Statutes of Nevada,* Twentieth Session (1901), chapter L, pp. 61–64.

[26] *Reno Evening Gazette,* July 3, 1901, p. 1.

[27] 111 *Federal Reporter,* 1902, pp. 71–81; *Central Pacific Railway Company v. Evans et al.* August 21, 1901.

[28] *Nevada State Journal,* August 14, 1901, p. 2; August 17, 1901, p. 2.

[29] *Morning Appeal,* August 24, 1901, p. 2.

[30] *Ibid.,* March 27, 1901, p. 2.

[31] See, e.g., *Nevada State Journal,* September 29, 1901, p. 2.

[32] Francis G. Newlands to Henry C. Hansbrough, February 4, 1901. Newlands papers.

[33] William Stewart to J. E. Stubbs, January 10, 1902. Stewart papers.

[34] William Stewart to James H. Marriott, Osceola, Nevada, January 24, 1902. Stewart papers.

[35] Francis Newlands to George Nixon, June 17, 1902. Newlands papers.

[36] William Stewart to *Carson News,* July 10, 1902. Stewart papers.

[37] Francis G. Newlands to William Sharon, December 28, 1901; Newlands to Sharon, May 10, 1902. Newlands papers.

[38] John H. Dennis to William E. Sharon, March 4, 1902; Dennis to Sharon, March 7, 1902. Newlands papers.

[39] *Nevada State Journal,* July 30, 1901, p. 2.

[40] *Ibid.,* August 14, 1901, p. 2.

[41] *Ibid.,* October 29, 1901, p. 2.

[42] *Ibid.,* November 16, 1901, p. 2.

[43] William E. Sharon to Francis G. Newlands, January 28, 1902. Newlands papers.

[44] See, e.g., *Nevada State Journal,* February 28, 1902, pp. 1 and 2.

[45] *Nevada State Journal,* March 11, 1902, p. 2; March 25, 1902, p. 2.

[46] *Ibid.,* April 13, 1902, p. 4.

[47] Francis G. Newlands to William E. Sharon, April 15, 1902. Newlands papers.

[48] George Nixon to Francis G. Newlands, May 3, 1902. Newlands papers.

[49] *Nevada State Journal,* May 16, 1902, p. 4.

[50] George T. Mills to William Stewart, June 9, 1902. Stewart papers.

[51] *Reno Evening Gazette,* July 25, 1902, p. 2.

[52] William Stewart to W. F. Herrin, August 8, 1902. Stewart papers.

[53] S. J. Andersen, Winnemucca, Nevada, to William Stewart, July 28, 1902. Stewart papers.

[54] William Stewart to Thomas P. Hawley, August 8, 1902. Stewart papers.

[55] *Nevada State Journal,* August 17, 1902, p. 4.

[56] *Ibid.,* August 13, 1902, p. 4.

[57] *Ibid.,* July 31, 1902, p. 4.

[58] *Reno Evening Gazette,* July 25, 1902, p. 2.

[59] Fred T. Dubois to John Sparks, July 4, 1902; Francis G. Newlands to Dubois, July 5, 1902. Newlands papers.

[60] *Reno Evening Gazette,* July 20, 1900, p. 2.

[61] William E. Sharon to Francis G. Newlands, March 7, 1902; Sharon to Newlands, February 18, 1902. Newlands papers.

[62] *Reno Evening Gazette,* November 4, 1950, p. 9.

[63] *Ibid.,* July 28, 1902, p. 3; *Nevada State Journal,* July 27, 1902, p. 1.

[64] *Reno Evening Gazette,* August 26, 1902, p. 4; *Nevada State Journal,* August 27, 1902, p. 1.

[65] *Nevada State Journal* and *Reno Evening Gazette,* August 26 to August 28, 1902, *passim.*

[66] Typescript in Newlands papers.

[67] *Reno Evening Gazette,* September 12 and September 13, 1902, *passim.*

[68] *Ibid.,* October 25, 1902, pp. 2 and 4.

[69] *Ibid.,* October 10, 1902, p. 2.

[70] *Ibid.,* October 9, 1902, p. 3.

[71] Nevada, Secretary of State, *Political History of Nevada, 1965,* p. 187.

[72] George T. Mills to William Stewart, November 10, 1902. Stewart papers.

IX

Epilogue

THE SILVER PARTY of Nevada remained nominally in existence through the 1906 election, but was never after 1902 more than a diminishing faction of the Democratic party. The Democrats took over the Silvermen so completely that the "fusion" ticket of 1904 and again of 1906 was designated "Democrat-Silver," instead of "Silver-Democrat," as it had been earlier. The last time any independent Silverman ran for office in Nevada was in 1904, when Reinhold Sadler tried to be elected to Congress on a "Stalwart Silver" ticket. He received only 572 votes. The presidential electors on the Stalwart Silver ticket that year—with conservatives in control of the national Democratic party—received fewer votes than Sadler. When William Jennings Bryan ran for president in 1908, some Nevada men styled themselves Silver-Democrats, but only the Democrats nominated electors pledged to their champion.

The silver issue, however, continued to be important in

Nevada politics for several years. Until nearly the middle of the twentieth century, no politician could survive if he failed to give lip service to some form of increased coinage of silver. Until George W. Malone entered the United States Senate in 1947, no clever politician endorsed the single gold standard. In the cause of the white metal, Nevada's representatives continued to be known as "silver senators."

Key Pittman was perhaps the outstanding example of the silver senator in the twentieth century. He was successful in promoting an act to assure miners a minimum price for silver bullion, and he pressed avidly for aid to the metal. Other Nevada representatives also upheld the local cause, but with diminishing zeal and effectiveness, until, in 1965, the silver content of United States coins was drastically reduced over almost unheard objections from western senators and congressmen. Certainly no one in 1965 seriously considered or advocated forming a new political party to obtain "justice for silver."

The associations that grew out of the Silver party contained a number of interesting factors for Nevada politics. The state's famous bipartisanship—the practice of attempting to elect one senator from each major party—may have had its prelude in 1904. George Nixon was elected to the United States Senate that year as a Republican, to join the Democratic senior senator, Newlands. Nixon's business partner, George Wingfield, promoted the bipartisan concept throughout his long tenure as a Nevada kingmaker. The Democrats, however, had made the state their own. In marked contrast to the political structure before 1892, the Democrats now normally elected their men with little difficulty, while the Republicans had only occasional success.

The changes stemmed from the councils that led to the organization of the Silver party of Nevada. When the Democrats stayed with the silver cause through the lean years of the 1890s, they did so to their own ultimate benefit. Republicans who might have remained loyal were effectively prevented from entering wholly into the cause by the national GOP position. There were other causes for continuing Democratic control—the dying out of Civil War partisanship, the absorption of organized labor into the Democratic party, the rise of the New Deal—but the vigor of the party in Nevada began in the politics of the Silver decade.

APPENDIX I

The Depression in Nevada, 1883–1903

Year	Farm Animals: Average Price Each[a]					Farm Products: Average Prices[b]			Minerals[c]
	Milch cows ($)	Cattle ($)	Horses ($)	Sheep ($)	Swine ($)	Hay ($/ton)	Potatoes ($/bu.)	Wheat ($/bu.)	Gross yield ($)
1883	36.00	18.00	50.51	2.09	11.40	13.25	.75	1.10	7,617,173
1884	37.33	27.15	55.47	2.06	8.40	8.30	.70	1.00	6,832,607
1885	40.00	27.57	60.75	1.92	6.73	7.25	.65	.92	7,324,062
1886	39.00	23.55	61.13	4.55	4.55	7.40	.65	.75	6,944,965
1887	36.10	21.92	55.15	1.71	5.32	9.75	.78	.80	7,187,895
1888	35.00	18.00	51.43	1.91	5.30	10.83	.67	.92	8,828,010
1889	35.50	20.37	67.50	2.80	5.35	9.00	.65	.75	8,095,123
1890	30.00	14.53	55.30	1.89	5.30	9.75	.70	.86	6,895,512
1891	31.00	15.46	48.13	2.35	6.15	5.00	.50	.87	5,559,469
1892	27.50	14.77	42.80	2.49	6.82	7.00	.58	.75	3,464,502
1893	30.00	15.59	40.00	2.43	6.86	10.00	.40	.73	3,001,678
1894	29.30	12.97	23.60	2.14	8.75	7.25	.35[d]	.75	1,995,830[d]
1895	14.00[d]	10.79[d]	23.62	2.42	3.80[d]	6.75	.38	.49[d]	2,104,550
1896	24.50	12.07	18.68	1.71	6.26	4.82[d]	.38	.69	3,480,102
1897	26.80	16.32	18.06	1.69[d]	5.09	5.00	.73	.90	3,628,190
1898	27.85	17.04	12.82	2.20	3.94	7.00	.90	.95	3,141,090
1899	29.25	19.80	11.94[d]	2.21	4.54	7.65	.90	.76	2,716,096
1900	34.10	23.06	16.41	2.91	5.67	7.70	.56	.70	2,632,923
1901	37.12	21.81	18.70	3.10	6.99	7.92	.91	.88	2,754,736
1902	39.08	21.37	30.16	2.73	6.44	9.05	.63	.98	3,366,607
1903	37.33	22.35	34.94	2.89	7.00	9.97	.70	.99	2,832,821

[a]U.S. Department of Agriculture, "Number and Farm Value of Farm Animals in the United States, 1867–1907," *Bureau of Statistics Bulletin No. 64* (1908).

[b]U.S. Department of Agriculture, "Hay Crops of the United States, 1866–1906," *Bureau of Statistics Bulletin No. 63* (1908). U.S. Department of Agriculture, "Potato Crops of the United States, 1866–1906," *Bureau of Statistics Bulletin No. 62* (1908). U.S. Department of Agriculture, "Wheat Crops of the United States, 1866–1907," *Bureau of Statistics Bulletin No. 57* (1907).

[c]Nevada Bureau of Mines, "Outline of Nevada Mining History," *Mackay School of Mines Report 7* (1964). The highest gross yield of mines in Nevada before 1916 was $46,671,870 (1877).

[d]Low point, 1883–1903.

APPENDIX II

POPULATION AND THE ELECTORATE IN NEVADA, 1880–1902

YEAR	POPULATION[a]	HIGHEST VOTE TALLIED[b]
1880	62,266	18,393
1882		14,359
1884		12,799
1886		12,374
1888		12,603
1890	47,355	12,408
1892		10,878
1894		10,473
1896		10,314
1898		10,008
1900	42,335	10,196
1902		11,318

[a]U.S. Bureau of the Census, *Population, Nevada.* 1880, 1890, 1900.
[b]Nevada Secretary of State, *Political History of Nevada, 1965.*

APPENDIX III

CONSTITUTION OF THE NEVADA SILVER ASSOCIATION, 1885

ARTICLE I.

SECTION 1. The Conventions of this Association shall be held annually, at such time and place as may be determined by a majority *viva voce* vote of all the members of the Association present, at any regular or called meeting. Should the Association for any cause fail to fix the time and place, then the President, or in his absence, the Vice President, shall cause the Secretary to issue a call for the Association to meet at some place to be designated in the call.

SECTION 2. The call provided for in Section one shall be issued at least thirty days prior to the date of holding the Convention, and shall be advertised in at least one newspaper published in each county represented in the Association. In the absence by death, resignation or otherwise, of the President and Vice-President, the Trustees, or a majority thereof, may direct the Secretary to make such call.

SECTION 3. A quorum for the transaction of business shall consist of at least twenty-five members.

ARTICLE II.

SECTION 1. Membership may be acquired during the sessions of the Association upon the recommendation of any member and a *viva voce* majority vote of all the members present; and during the annual recess of the Association, upon the recommendation of two members he may, in writing, countersigned by two members, make application to the Secretary and authorize said Secretary to sign the applicant's name to the Constitution.

SECTION 2. To enable persons who reside at a distance from the location of the Secretary to consummate membership, signing the Constitution in the manner provided in Section one of Article II, shall constitute membership in the Association.

ARTICLE III.

SECTION 1. Each applicant for membership shall pay into the Association as an admission fee, the sum of five dollars.

SECTION 2. Each member shall pay as annual dues, five dollars.

SECTION 3. Assessments may be levied when deemed expedient, by a majority of members present at any regular or called meeting of the Association.

ARTICLE IV.

SECTION 1.   The officers of the Association shall consist of a President, one Vice-President, one Secretary and one Treasurer, all of whom shall be elected annually and by a *viva voce* majority vote of all the members present.

SECTION 2.   The officers shall perform such duties as the Association may direct.

SECTION 3.   There shall be elected annually three Trustees, who shall perform such duties as the Association may direct.

SECTION 4.   There shall be elected annually a Finance Committee, to consist of three members, whose duty it shall be to attend to all matters of a financial nature that may be referred to them.

ARTICLE V.

SECTION 1.   The Association may make such by-laws as are deemed necessary, and not in conflict with this Constitution.

SECTION 2.   This Constitution may be amended at any regular or called meeting of the Association, by a *viva voce* vote of two-thirds of all the members present. The undersigned members of this Association hereby pledge themselves to maintain the principles announced in the foregoing Constitution.

Bibliography

PUBLIC DOCUMENTS

Humboldt County, Nevada. Assessor. Assessment Books, 1891, 1892. Nevada State Archives, Carson City, Nevada.

Nevada. Bureau of Mines. *Outline of Nevada Mining History.* Mackay School of Mines, Report 7 (1964).

Nevada. Secretary of State. *Political History of Nevada, 1965.* Carson City: State Printing Office, 1965.

Nevada. State Legislature. *Appendix to the Journals of the Senate and Assembly,* 1893, 1895, 1897, 1899, 1901.

.... *Journal of the Assembly,* 1899, 1901.

.... *Journal of the Senate,* 1895, 1899, 1901.

.... *Statutes of Nevada,* 1895, 1897, 1899, 1901.

Nevada. Surveyor General. *Biennial Report of the Surveyor General and State Land Register,* 1887–1895.

Proceedings of the Nevada Silver Convention Held at Carson City, Nevada, January 31, 1885. Carson City: J. C. Harlow, State Printer, 1885.

U.S. *Congressional Globe.* Forty-second Congress, 3rd session, 1873.

U.S. Department of Agriculture. *Hay Crops of the United States, 1866–1906.* Bureau of Statistics Bulletin No. 63 (1908).

.... *Number and Farm Value of Farm Animals in the United States, 1867–1907.* Bureau of Statistics Bulletin No. 64 (1908).

.... *Potato Crops of the United States, 1866–1906.* Bureau of Statistics Bulletin No. 62 (1908).

.... *Wheat Crops of the United States, 1866–1907.* Bureau of Statistics Bulletin No. 57 (1907).

U.S. *Federal Reporter.* Volume 111, 1902.

Washoe County, Nevada. Assessor. Assessment Books, 1891, 1892. Nevada State Archives, Carson City, Nevada.

BOOKS

Angel, Myron, ed. *History of the State of Nevada.* Berkeley: Howell-North Books, 1958. Photo reprint of 1881 edition by Thompson and West.

Bryan, William Jennings. *First Battle: A Story of the Campaign of 1896.* Chicago: W. B. Conkey Company, 1896.

Buchanan, A. Russell. *David S. Terry of California: Dueling Judge.* San Marino: The Huntington Library, 1956.

Buck, Solon Justus. *The Agrarian Crusade: A Chronicle of the Farmer in Politics.* New Haven: Yale University Press, 1920.

Byars, William Vincent, ed. *An American Commoner: The Life and Times of Richard Parks Bland.* Columbus, Missouri: E. W. Stephens, 1900.

Davis, Samuel Post, ed. *The History of Nevada.* 2 vols. Reno: The Elms Publishing Company, 1913.

Elliott, Russell R. *Nevada's Twentieth-Century Mining Boom.* Reno: University of Nevada Press, 1966.

Friedman, Milton, and Anna Jacobsen Schwartz. *A Monetary History of the United States, 1867–1960.* Princeton: Princeton University Press, 1963.

Glad, Paul W. *The Trumpet Soundeth: William Jennings Bryan and His Democracy, 1896–1912.* Lincoln: Uuniversity of Nebraska Press, 1960.

Hicks, John Donald. *The Populist Revolt: A History of the Farm-*

er's Alliance and the People's Party. Minneapolis: University of Minnesota Press, 1931.

Hollingsworth, J. Rogers. *The Whirligig of Politics: The Democracy of Cleveland and Bryan.* Chicago: University of Chicago Press, 1963.

Myrick, David F. *Railroads of Nevada and Eastern California.* 2 vols. Berkeley: Howell-North Books, 1963.

National Cyclopaedia of American Biography. New York: James T. White and Company, 1909. Vol. XI.

Ostrander, Gilman. *Nevada, The Great Rotten Borough, 1859–1964.* New York: Alfred A. Knopf, 1966.

Porter, Kirk H., and Donald Bruce Johnson, comps. *National Party Platforms, 1840–1956.* Urbana: University of Illinois Press, 1956.

Scrugham, James G., ed. *Nevada.* 3 vols. Chicago: American Historical Society, 1935.

Shannon, Fred A. *The Farmer's Last Frontier* (Vol. 5 of *The Economic History of the United States*). New York: Rinehart and Company, 1945.

Sherman, John. *John Sherman's Recollections of Forty Years in the House, Senate, and Cabinet.* Chicago: The Werner Company, 1895. Popular edition.

Stewart, William Morris. *Analysis of the Functions of Money.* Washington, D.C.: William Ballantyne and Sons, 1898.

.... *Reminiscences of Senator William M. Stewart of Nevada.* Edited by George Rothwell Brown. New York: The Neale Publishing Company, 1908.

Swisher, Carl Brent. *Stephen J. Field: Craftsman of the Law.* Washington, D.C.: The Brookings Institution, 1930.

Tugwell, Rexford G. *Grover Cleveland.* New York: The Macmillan Company, 1968.

ARTICLES AND NEWSPAPERS

Carson Morning News (Carson City, Nevada), September 13 and 16, 1894.

Daily Independent (Elko, Nevada), September, 1892.

Davis, Samuel Post. "Political Revolution in Nevada," *San Francisco Call,* November 3, 1895.

Delamar Lode (Delamar, Nevada), February 7, 1899.

Eureka Daily Sentinel (Eureka, Nevada), October and November, 1886.

Genoa Weekly Courier (Genoa, Nevada), August 19, 1892.

Helena Independent (Helena, Montana), July 16, 1892.

Jones, John Percival. "The Remonetization of Silver," Speech by the Hon. John P. Jones in the Senate of the United States, October 14, 16, 21, 23, 24, 27, and 30, 1893.

Mack, Effie Mona. "William Morris Stewart, 1827–1909," *Nevada Historical Society Quarterly,* VII (1964).

Morning Appeal (Carson City, Nevada), January, 1885; September, 1889, through June, 1892; September, 1894; August, 1898, through March, 1901; August 24, 1901.

Myles, Myrtle. "Fortune for a Governor," *Las Vegas Review-Journal,* May 24, 1964.

Nevada State Journal (Reno, Nevada), January through May, 1890; March, 1891; May through June, 1892; January, 1893; January through March, 1895; January through March, 1897; July, 1898, through March, 1899; April, 1900; August 31, 1900; 1901; February through August, 1902.

New York Times, December 18, 1895; June 19 and 20, 1896; January 21, 1899; March 11, 20, and 28, 1899; April 21, 1899; July 3 and 4, 1900.

Reno Evening Gazette (Reno, Nevada), June, 1892; July through October, 1894; October, 1895; August and September, 1896; December 15, 1896; March through June, 1897; August through October, 1898; April through October, 1900; January through July, 1901; July through October, 1902; January 29, 1906; November 4, 1950.

Reno Weekly Gazette and Stockman, January 3, 1889; March 16, 1893.

San Francisco Call, November 3, 1895.

San Francisco Chronicle, January 31, 1901.

San Francisco Examiner, November 1, 1896; January 7, 1899.

Silver State (Winnemucca, Nevada), September 21 and 26, 1878;

May 12 and 28, 1880; September 6 and 7, 1882; May 3, 1884; June 11, 1884; September, 1886; May through June, 1890; 1892–1897.

Territorial Enterprise (Virginia City, Nevada), December 18, 1872; February 4, 1873; February 27, 1895; August 31, 1900; September 7, 1900.

Weekly Independent (Elko, Nevada), September 13 and 21, 1896.

Weekly Sentinel (Eureka, Nevada), April 16, 1892; February 2, 1901.

Weinstein, Allen. "Was There a 'Crime of 1873'?: The Case of the Demonetized Dollar," *Journal of American History*, LIV:2 (September, 1967), 307–326.

.... "The Bonanza King Myth: Western Mine Owners and the Remonetization of Silver," *Business History Review* XLII:2 (Summer, 1968), 195–218.

White Pine News (Ely, Nevada), August 23, 1890.

UNPUBLISHED MATERIALS

Coffin, Trenmor. Papers. University of Nevada Library, Reno.

Crowell, Lucy Davis. "One Hundred Years at Nevada's Capital." Typescript of oral history interview, conducted by Mary Ellen Glass for the Oral History Project of the Center for Western North American Studies, University of Nevada, 1965. University of Nevada Library, Reno.

Gallagher, Charles D. "Autobiography and Reminiscence." Typescript of oral history interview, conducted by Mary Ellen Glass for the Oral History Project of the Center for Western North American Studies, University of Nevada, 1965. University of Nevada Library, Reno.

Governor's Office Letter Book (Jones, Sadler, Allen, Sparks). Nevada Historical Society, Reno.

Governor's Office Letter Box, 1897–1899. Nevada Historical Society.

Gulling, Amy T. "An Interview With Amy Gulling." Typescript of oral history interview, conducted by Mary Ellen Glass for the Oral History Project of the Center for Western North American Studies, University of Nevada, 1966. University of Nevada Library, Reno.

Hilp, Lester J. "Reminiscences of a White Pine County Native, Reno Pharmacy Owner, and Civic Leader." Typescript of oral history interview, conducted by Mary Ellen Glass for the Oral History Project of the Center for Western North American Studies, University of Nevada, 1967. University of Nevada Library, Reno.

Letters to the Governor's Office, 1893–1898. Letter box. Nevada Historical Society.

Newlands, Francis Griffith. Papers. Yale University Library, New Haven, Connecticut (microfilm at University of Nevada Library, Reno).

Scheidler, Lawrence John. "Silver and Politics, 1893–1896." Ph.D. dissertation, Indiana University, 1936.

Stewart, William Morris. Papers. Nevada Historical Society.

Report of the State Auditing Committee of the Silver Party of Nevada, 1898. Nevada Historical Society.

Index